Met baie liefde

aan

Johan, Anita, Janus en Esmari

van

Pappa en Mamma,
Christo,
Ockert en Bokkie,
Hannes, Mariaan, Tiaan en Jacques.

LEKKER LEES !!

THE SECRET
ELEPHANTS

THE SECRET ELEPHANTS

The rediscovery of the world's most southerly elephants

GARETH PATTERSON

PENGUIN BOOKS

PENGUIN BOOKS

Published by the Penguin Group
Penguin Books (South Africa) (Pty) Ltd, 24 Sturdee Avenue, Rosebank, Johannesburg 2196, South Africa
Penguin Group (USA) Inc, 375 Hudson Street, New York, New York 10014, USA
Penguin Group (Canada), 90 Eglinton Avenue East, Suite 700, Toronto, Ontario, Canada M4P 2Y3 (a division of Pearson Penguin Canada Inc)
Penguin Books Ltd, 80 Strand, London WC2R 0RL, England
Penguin Ireland, 25 St Stephen's Green, Dublin 2, Ireland (a division of Penguin Books Ltd)
Penguin Group (Australia), 250 Camberwell Road, Camberwell, Victoria 3124, Australia (a division of Pearson Australia Group Pty Ltd)
Penguin Books India Pvt Ltd, 11 Community Centre, Panchsheel Park, New Delhi – 110 017, India
Penguin Group (NZ), 67 Apollo Drive, Mairangi Bay, Auckland 1310, New Zealand (a division of Pearson New Zealand Ltd)

Penguin Books (South Africa) (Pty) Ltd, Registered Offices:
24 Sturdee Avenue, Rosebank, Johannesburg 2196, South Africa

www.penguinbooks.co.za

First published by Penguin Books (South Africa) (Pty) Ltd 2009

ISBN 9780143026136

Typeset by Nix Design in 11.5/14.5 pt IowanOld
Cover Michiel Botha
Cover photograph by Patty Ghillebert
Printed and bound by CTP Book Printers, Cape Town

Contents

PART FOUR

Foreword

Dr Dame Daphne Sheldrick DBE MBE MBS DVMS
1992 Global 500 Laureate

Initially, it was with mixed feelings that I agreed to write this Foreword to Gareth Patterson's moving exposure about the secretive and mysterious existence of the elephant survivors within the beautiful Knysna forest. Aware of the tribulation and suffering of elephants generally at the hands of humans, my first feeling was one of sadness, that perhaps it would have been better had their existence remained a mystery for in that way they would be spared the intrusion of human curiosity that usually leads to harassment in the name of Science. But, upon reflection, I felt that perhaps it was inevitable that their existence become known, and what more sensitive person than my friend Gareth Patterson to bring their existence and plight to the attention of the world, and by so doing appeal to the good in caring humankind to afford them the privacy and shelter they have carved out for themselves over the years. How desperately sad it would have been had the Matriarch of such a highly social species lived all alone in her forested stronghold, with no one to love and protect and with whom to talk, all things we know that elephants do. As it is, Gareth Patterson has documented their secret world with empathy and understanding, as one who regards himself in harmony with it. Few could have done this with more perception than Gareth, and I hope that his moving narrative will ensure that the Knysna elephants are viewed with wonder and awe as a national and international treasure, symbolic of endurance against all odds, as well as symbolic of the precarious nature of their beleaguered species.

I have been privileged to come to know elephants well for I have worked intimately with them for fifty out of my three score years and ten, having retrieved and reared their broken orphaned babies and gradually watched them return to where they rightly belong, back amongst their own kind in a protected area that can afford them the space an elephant needs for a quality of life. I have shed tears of sorrow aplenty as well as tears of joy for them and their kind. They have taught me and my colleagues well, and continue to do so on a daily basis as we follow the lives of the seventy-four orphaned elephants we have hand-reared from early infancy, many of whom are now grown and have wild-born young of their own, living unfettered and free amongst Kenya's largest single elephant population. We have healed the physical wounds of the orphans that have come to us, and watched with wonder and awe at the healing of deep-seated psychological scars brought about by the compassion and comfort of their orphaned peers and we have marvelled at their forgiveness. To have been befriended by elephants is a humbling and unique experience filled with wonder, awe and amazement, for every day brings new revelations about these wonderful, very 'human' animals. Their care of one another, and their understanding and compassion are surely an example of the very best of human traits; their gentle nature and forgiveness tempers justifiable resentment and anger against humans who deprived them of their loved elephant family. On numerous occasions we have witnessed first hand their mysterious perception of hidden dangers no human could have detected ahead of time. We have also seen them healing themselves through self-medication, the selection of offered medicinal essential oils and plants, something that has been documented scientifically by specialists in this field. We have observed how they can communicate a sophisticated message to one another, how unconditional and unselfish is their love of the young irrespective of age, how deeply they mourn a lost loved one, and how they bury their dead, covering them with sticks and leaves, returning periodically to reflect and remember. We have marvelled how a completely wild elephant has stood vigil over a blind man who lost his way in the wilderness, ensuring his safety until dawn brought a relative to retrieve him. We have witnessed our orphaned Matriarch save, protect and keep a night-long watch over an old buffalo wounded by a pride of lions, driving off the pride at great risk to herself and standing guard over the victim until dawn lit the sky. All these things and much, much more have left us all with a deep respect and love for these incredible animals.

That elephants are highly sophisticated, mysteriously intelligent, and *never forget* is no myth, but a truth. Since an elephant can read one's mind and heart, we know that they can recognise and discern between human individuals who have treated them with kindness and care, and those that regard them as a commodity, their only worth what they can bring in monetary remuneration. With elephants, one reaps what one sows, and Gareth Patterson through his beautiful book has sown the seeds of love and understanding of the wonderfully mysterious and secretive remnant Knysna elephant community. It is our prayer that they remain protected and secluded in their beautiful forest stronghold.

I was particularly moved by the truth of Gareth Patterson's words that humans, having damaged the earth, tainted the water, poisoned the air, and changed the climate, now have an obligation to protect the last remaining bastions of true wilderness and the animal lives these wondrous places harbour within. Mankind cannot exist in isolation of the natural world. The remarkable discoveries he has made about the mysterious endurance of those few elephant fugitives that have found each other and shelter in the secret places deep within the Knysna forest, against all odds, are a testimony to endurance and continuity.

Author's Note

Although the African lion has been the focus of my adult life, elephants have always loomed closely in the background. When I studied lions in the wilds of Botswana, when I worked with George Adamson of *Born Free* fame, and when I rehabilitated George's last lion orphans back into the wilds and lived as a human member of a lion pride, elephants were always present in my life. Then, six years ago, a series of events and circumstances steered me to focus completely on elephants for a while. I began an independent field study of a mysterious elephant population on the southern tip of Africa, the secret elephants of Knysna.

The very existence of these elephants defies probability. It has been estimated that when the European settlers arrived on the shores of the Cape more than three hundred years ago, some one hundred thousand elephants may have existed in what is today the Republic of South Africa. By 1870, this elephant population had virtually been wiped out by professional ivory hunters, sportsmen, and settler farmers. By 1910 less than two hundred elephants, in four separate fragmented populations, remained. The southern-most of these populations were the elephants of Knysna in the southern Cape. In 1969, just eleven of these elephants were still alive.

In recent years the local forestry department declared that the elephants were confined to the dense Knysna forest, an unsuitable habitat for savannah elephants, and that poor nutrition in the forest had resulted in very low reproduction rates. Hence it was stated that the declining numbers were merely the result of the dying out of old elephants. Others disagreed sharply with this hypothesis, though, citing illegal hunting and ineffectual conservation as the true causes of the Knysna elephants' continued demise in recent decades.

In 1994 it was stated that only one Knysna elephant was still alive, a mysterious elderly female known as 'The Matriarch'.

The world's southern-most elephant population was then described as being 'functionally extinct'.[1]

After covering thousands of kilometres on foot during the past six years, walking the ancient pathways of ghostly giants through forests and on the slopes of mountains, I learnt that it was not the end for the Knysna elephants. I discovered that other, previously unknown Knysna elephants exist secretly. And these are young adult elephants – elephants, it seems, that developed unique survival strategies that enabled them to come back from the very brink . . .

This is the story of these remarkable elephants.

---

[1] Dudley, J P (1999). African Elephants in Coastal Refuges: Postscript. *Pachyderm* 22.

PART ONE

O N E

If Silence Could Speak

*I cannot omit their care, to bury and cover the dead carcasses of their companions,
or any others of their kind; for finding them dead they pass not by them till they
have lamented their common misery, by casting dust and earth on them, and
also green boughs, in token of sacrifice . . .*
Parson and naturalist, Edward Topsell
Historie of the Foure-Footed Beasts, 1607

6 March 1999
The Knysna Forests

Something had gone dreadfully wrong. The green Bell Jet Ranger
helicopter had been flying due west along the beautiful southern Cape
coast of South Africa. The pilot made radio contact with flight control
at 4.15pm. It was a clear day, with ideal flying conditions.

The helicopter was seen by forest workers as it flew over the Diepwalle
forest station at 4.30pm.

Then it simply disappeared.

Four days after its mysterious disappearance there was still no sign
of the helicopter, despite extensive ground and aerial searches. The
following day the search was continued, and then again on the day
after. Three different helicopters, including an Oryx helicopter from

the South African Air Force, flew transects across the forests and mountains, but nothing was found. Not a single sign. It was as if the helicopter had vanished from the face of the earth.

Concerned members of the public used Internet postings to encourage anyone entering the Knysna forest to maintain vigilance, and to look out for signs of the helicopter or crash site. One such message on an ornithology website read:

> Subject: Missing Helicopter, Area: Knysna Forest. PLEASE HELP. If any of you are birding in this area in the future, PLEASE could you keep a lookout for a helicopter that went missing on the 6th of this month, which still has not been found. Please take note of any unusual smells, dying trees, gathering birds such as flycatchers, drongos, or any carrion eaters i.e. crows, raptors etc.
>
> There is a substantial reward for anyone who finds it. The details are: Bell Jet Ranger ZS-REB, green on top, white underneath with thin yellow stripe between. Last positive sighting was from the Diepwalle forest station in the Knysna forest.

❖

It was dusk when the lone elderly female elephant found the helicopter. The Matriarch raised her trunk and smelt the fuel-laden air. She then stepped towards the crashed aircraft.

For days now other helicopters had flown low over the forest in search of the fallen aircraft, towards which the Matriarch was now slowly moving. The forest had, it seemed, simply swallowed up all signs of the crash from the eyes of humanity.

It lay there, in front of her, like a broken and twisted metallic whale. At first, the Matriarch stood in silence, completely still, apart from her trunk which was smelling the ground. Then she reached out and touched the green-coloured fuselage with the tip of her trunk. Three people had died at this place.

The Matriarch shifted her weight and began digging at the ground with her front right foot, cupping the soil and leaves with her trunk before sprinkling them on to the helicopter. She continued doing this for many minutes. Then she slowly turned and began to break branches from the trees, which she used to partially cover the helicopter, and the dead.

This was elephant burial ritual. They do this when one of their kind dies. Mysteriously, they also do this when one of our kind dies. They bury their kind . . . and ours.

❖

A few days after the helicopter went missing I gave a presentation on how, after the murder of my friend George Adamson, I had rescued George's last lion orphans in Kenya, and returned them to the wilds in the Tuli bushlands of Botswana. The audience that evening consisted of South African businessmen and their wives.

During the presentation I mentioned that I occasionally used a divining technique, with a map and a pendulum, as a means of locating lions. In principle this is similar to the way in which people divine for water. Dowsing, as it is called, is one of the oldest arts and is widely used today in fields as diverse as medicine and archaeology. George Adamson's brother Terence discovered late in his life that he could locate George's lions, geological faults, and even missing people, with the use of a pendulum and map.

After hearing about this method I, too, from time to time would use a pendulum to locate lions. I did not have Terence's accuracy, though. With me, the pendulum usually indicated where lions had been a day or so before, but this was still useful information and could be built on when tracking lions in the field.

After the lecture that evening, a woman came up to me. She was clearly racked with emotional pain and tears soon rimmed her eyes as she began telling me about a missing helicopter somewhere on the southern Cape coast. The people who had been aboard the helicopter were close friends of hers, Ian Macfarlane, his wife Frances and his father, Boyd Macfarlane. The woman asked if I would dowse for the helicopter. Of course, I said that I would try.

I did this the following day. Generally with dowsing, if the pendulum rotates in a clockwise direction it indicates that whoever you are searching for is alive. But when I placed a map of the southern Cape on a table, to my alarm, the pendulum swung anti-clockwise, indicating that death had occurred. The pendulum rotated in small tight circles over one particular point, and when I placed a pin at this point, I saw that it marked the centre of the Knysna forest, just south of a forest station called Diepwalle.

The pendulum had gravitated to the central range of the last Knysna elephants.

And this, in a sense, was my first direct 'connection' with the Knysna elephants. From that moment on, circumstances began to lead me towards the mysterious world of these elephants.

T W O

Burial Rituals

The signs from the pendulum looked grim, and I decided to leave the matter alone. I did not contact the woman, as ground and aerial searches were continuing. I could not tell her what the pendulum had indicated. I could not take away hope when hope still existed. After all, I could have been wrong. And how desperately I wish I had been.

From the time I first heard about the tragedy, I thought a lot about the missing helicopter and the Matriarch. I felt very strongly that the Matriarch could have gone to the crashed helicopter at some time, and performed what I can only describe as the elephant 'burial ritual' there.

With this in mind, I decided to contact the well-known elephant expert, Joyce Poole. She has studied elephants for the past thirty years and probably understands the mind and behaviour of the African elephant better than anyone else on earth.

I asked Joyce what she thought might have occurred after the helicopter had crashed into the Matriarch's forest.

Her answer was simple and unhesitating:

> I think that elephants might well have gone to the place, and covered the bodies, as well as portions of the helicopter, with branches. I

know of a similar situation, told to me by a colleague, a case he witnessed as a boy when an elephant killed his herding friend.

Joyce wrote poignantly about elephant burial behaviour in her book *Coming of Age with Elephants*:

> They reserve this behaviour for their own kind and sometimes, for one other species: humans. If elephants see themselves as different from the other animals, is it possible that they see humans as different from the rest of nature? And how do they measure that difference? If elephants have the capacity to think consciously, if they understand death, is there any indication that they can empathise?

Joyce's colleague Simon Makulla witnessed a human burial by elephants when he was a child growing up near the Maasai Mara Game Reserve in Kenya. Simon and his friend were herding cattle one afternoon when they suddenly came across an elephant. It immediately charged towards them, scattering the boys in opposite directions. Simon heard terrible screams. Then there was silence . . .

Simon cautiously made his way in the direction from which he had heard the screams. He saw the elephant standing over the still body of his friend. It was gently touching the boy's body. Then, using its trunk and forefoot, it began covering the boy with earth. When the body was completely covered, the elephant broke branches off nearby trees and placed them one by one over the mound covering the dead boy. When this was complete, the elephant stood quietly next to the body. At this point Simon ran away from the scene, back to his homestead. It was almost dark by the time he got home.

The following morning, elders from Simon's homestead went to the place where the young boy had been killed and buried by the elephant. There they saw the elephant, still standing in silence, beside the mound of earth and branches. They watched quietly before leaving the elephant to its lonely vigil.

The Maasai people have a tradition of placing vegetation into the orifices of any human skulls they come across in the bush. Perhaps, taking the above story into account, it is not strange to learn that the Maasai do the same whenever they encounter the skull of an elephant.

In her book *Elephant Memories* Cynthia Moss's description of the burial ritual of a young Amboseli female elephant known as Tina is eerily similar to that of the young boy. Poachers shot Tina in the chest. Despite having a bullet in her right lung, she had run back with her terrified herd in the direction of the Amboseli National Park.

But it was too much. Sadly, but almost inevitably bearing in mind the severe nature of her injury, she fell to her side. Then, with blood pouring from her mouth, Tina died.

Members of her family attempted to lift her upright, but her body flopped limply to the ground. Later, the burial ritual began. The elephants began digging the hard ground, and sprinkled earth over Tina's body. Some of the herd broke branches off low bushes and placed them on top of the carcass. By sunset Tina's body had been almost entirely covered. The elephants stayed at the place for almost the entire night. This, too, is part of the burial vigil of elephants – they remain for long periods with the dead, be they elephant or human.

Finally, the elephants moved away.

One night at Kampi ya Simba in Kenya's Kora Game Reserve, George Adamson told me a strange tale about elephants burying a person. George was convinced that elephants understood the concept of death and that, as Joyce implies, they experience a kind of empathy when encountering dead humans.

'There are many well-known cases of elephants burying people they killed, burying them under wood and branches,' George said to me that night. He went on to tell me the following story.

> One evening a tracker of mine, Gobus, was returning to his home with his elderly mother after visiting friends at a village. After walking some distance, Gobus had to attend to a call of nature. He

told his mother to continue on the path, saying that he would catch up with her. His mother was half-blind and strayed off the path and became lost. As it was getting dark, she resigned herself to see the night through by staying beneath a tree. Later she fell asleep but awoke some time later to find an elephant standing over her. It was gently touching her skin. Terrified, she remained motionless. Other elephants then appeared and, trumpeting loudly, began tearing down branches and placing them on top of her.

By this time, Gobus had reached home and found that his mother was not there. It was dark by then and he could only begin searching for her at daybreak the following morning. The next day a man herding livestock heard faint calls for help. He found the elderly woman unhurt, but imprisoned under the pile of branches.

'I think,' George said to me, as he puffed on his pipe, 'I think the elephants must have thought she was dead . . .'

❖

I cannot prove that the Matriarch or any other Knysna elephant went to the site of the crashed helicopter. But should an elephant have done so, I feel, as Joyce did, that a burial ritual would have taken place.

Four months after the helicopter tragedy, I was exploring the Knysna forests for the very first time. On reflection, in some strange way it almost seems that after dowsing for the missing helicopter, I was being drawn to learn about the secret elephants of Knysna.

T H R E E

The Forest of Secret Voices

I had seen a herd of elephant travelling through dense native forest, where the sunlight is strewn down between the thick creepers in small spots and patches, pacing along as if they had an appointment at the end of the world.
Isak Dinesen
Out of Africa, 1937

In July 1999, my then girlfriend Fransje van Riel and I visited the southern Cape to make plans for the establishment of a sanctuary for four lions that could not be rehabilitated back into the wilds. Today this natural habitat sanctuary, Lion Haven, exists on a plateau overlooking the Indian Ocean some 70 kilometres from where I am now writing these words at the edge of the Knysna forest.

With the planning for the establishment of Lion Haven complete, Fransje and I decided to drive east along the coast to the Knysna area. This is a coastline of great natural beauty, a microcosm of any of the earth's coastal regions. It is a place of dunes, great rocky cliffs, deep gorges, seashore, estuaries, mountains and lakes. It is also a place famous for its forests and, of course, the mysterious Knysna elephants. To the east the indigenous forest stretches inland from cliffs high above the crashing ocean waves. And beyond the forests, like a vast sentinel looking over the land, stands the Outeniqua mountain range. The story of the Knysna elephants first became internationally known through the historical novel *Circles in a Forest* written by Dalene Matthee. Set in the 1880s, *Circles in a Forest* told of one man's fight to save the Knysna elephants and the great forest through which they roamed. The novel, first published in 1984, was a literary sensation, resulting in empathy and concern for the last Knysna elephants, the most southerly elephants in the world.

On that first day in the Knysna area, we set out to explore a portion of the forest in the early afternoon, driving north, and inland from the holiday town of Knysna. Before entering the indigenous forest, we first drove through the commercial pine plantations. And it was here that we encountered a troop of baboons. It was a curious and incongruous sight, the baboons among trees from another land.

After leaving the baboons, we plunged into the dense, magnificent indigenous forest, a cool, quiet, leafy place. Less than one per cent of the total land area of South Africa is indigenous forest, the country being largely arid. But here, on the southern tip of the country, there are some 600 square kilometres of luxuriant Afromontane forest.

Everything was completely new to me. Shafts of lemon sunlight illuminated splashes of the otherwise dark interior. I knew virtually nothing about this African interior. What I did know, though, was that it was a magical place . . .

A little later, we passed a large green sign deep in the forest that shouted:

DANGER!
You are now entering an area where elephants roam wild.
ENTER AT YOUR OWN RISK!

Further along the road we passed another sign, indicating the turn-off to the Diepwalle forest station.

'Diepwalle,' I mused. 'Part of the haunts of the Matriarch, the elderly, lone female.'

This was the very locality my pendulum had centred on four months earlier when I dowsed for the missing helicopter.

In 1994, in a bold experiment to boost the numbers of the last Knysna elephants, three orphaned 'cull' female elephants from the Kruger National Park were brought to these forests. At the time it was thought that the Matriarch, an old bull, and a younger bull of about twenty-four years, were the very last Knysna elephants. But no one was sure about this. Nothing about these mysterious elephants seemed to have been positively ascertained.

Three months after the arrival of the Kruger orphans, but just before their release into the forest from the fenced holding area in which they were initially kept, doubts arose as to whether the three Knysna elephants existed at all. In those three months there had not been a single sign that any of the Knysna elephants had approached the vicinity of the holding area. This was thought to be strange (and rightly so), for surely the presence of these new elephants would have attracted resident Knysna elephants to the holding area.

As a result, an intensive search was launched with forest guards and workers combing large areas of the main forest. Only one Knysna elephant was found – the lone Matriarch. It was then widely assumed that the Knysna elephants were a doomed population. The Kruger orphans were all females, thus their release into the forests would mean there would be an all-female population.

Shortly after the release of the Kruger orphans from their holding area, the youngest female, probably no more than eight years old, was found dead in the forest. It was said that she had died of stress-related pneumonia.

The two remaining orphans later joined up with the Matriarch, and for almost two months the three elephants moved together as a small herd, with the Matriarch introducing the orphans to the forest and the mountain fynbos[2] country to the north-east. The grand old lady of the forest put aside her solitary life in order to settle the orphans

---

[2] The Cape fynbos makes up four-fifths of the Cape Floral Kingdom, the smallest of the world's six floral kingdoms. Described as a wonder of the world, the Cape Floral Kingdom comprises some 8 600 diverse plant species, of which about 5 800 are endemic and exist nowhere else.

into their new environment. One comes to expect this sort of thing from elephants.

The time came when the Matriarch returned to her usual haunts, leaving behind the orphans, who increasingly roamed the fynbos areas on the foothills of the Outeniqua Mountains, to the north beyond the forest.

For most of the next four years, the young elephants lived in this area where, according to Wilfred Oraai and Karel Maswatie, two forest guards who monitored the Kruger orphans' movements on foot, they seemed very happy. The orphans had adapted well to their new environment, but ultimately they were destined to be recaptured and removed from their adopted home.

As we drove through the Knysna forest that day in July 1999, I pondered the situation. Unless an unknown bull existed, it seemed like the end for this relic elephant population that had been defiant for so long.

Already ideas were forming in my mind as I wondered how I might be able to attempt to do something for these last elephants on the southern tip of Africa. Perhaps I could search for others; for previously unknown Knysna elephants. Could there be a bull out there? Perhaps it was not the end for the elephants on the edge of the world. Elephants on the edge . . . .

We drove on slowly until the dense indigenous forest gave way to pine plantations. In a high open area I pulled the car to one side of the road and got out to look around. Towards the south I could see the ocean. Hundreds of square kilometres of indigenous forest and plantations surrounded me. To the north lay the grandeur of the Outeniqua Mountains. Surely, I said to myself, there must be other Knysna elephants somewhere out there. The place was vast. How could anyone be certain it was the end for these elephants?

I felt a surge of optimism before, suddenly, like a strange cloud, a sense of sadness descended upon me.

It was about four in the afternoon when we drove through the Gouna portion of the forest towards the town of Knysna.

I felt an increasing and inexplicable uneasiness that evening in our hotel room, with sadness welling up within me. I did not understand what was affecting me so badly. Fransje was very disturbed by my mood. Had I eaten something toxic? Had something poisonous bitten me while we were in the forest?

Eventually I fell asleep, but woke at intervals throughout the night. And, in the patches of sleep, I dreamt of terrified, running young elephants.

The following morning I woke up feeling exhausted, but still could not understand what had been wrong the evening before. It was to remain a mystery for the next four years.

F O U R

Capture of the Orphans

The elephant is said sometimes to weep
Charles Darwin

The two female Kruger orphans were removed from the foothills of the Outeniqua Mountains. Taken away from the place to which they had been brought, the place to which they had adapted, and which had been their home for almost five years. The capture of the orphans took place on 20 July 1999.

The Department of Water Affairs and Forestry had, 'in consultation with a panel of experts, including the National Parks Board, decided that the (Kruger) elephants will have to be removed'. And that the 'original long-term aim of resettling elephants in the Knysna forests would not be met any more . . .'[3]

One of the reasons given for removing the orphans was that they were no longer moving with the Matriarch, and because they preferred to live and feed in the mountain fynbos country rather than the forest. It was perceived that the orphans had not adapted to the forest environment. This perception was based on what people had expected the orphans would do when they were released – that they would stay with the Matriarch, and stay in the forest. After all, Knysna elephants, so it was thought at the time, were confined to the forest environment.

---

[3] *The Star* newspaper, 22 January 1997.

July 1999
Diepwalle forest station, Knysna

Since Friday 16 July, the game capture team had been attempting to locate and tranquillise the Kruger orphans. But the orphans' movements, combined with deteriorating weather conditions, were thwarting and frustrating the capture team's mission. Seemingly aware that they were being pursued, the orphans initially stayed within the pine plantations.

The following day they headed north, up on to the slopes of the Outeniqua Mountains and into rugged, isolated country, far from humans. It is the sort of country in which a person would seek refuge from a posse. There, up in the mountains, you would believe no one would ever find you.

By Monday, heavy sheets of rain veiled the orphans' presence on the mountainside, preventing any attempts at capture. It was as if the elements were trying to protect the orphans. The next day, high winds made helicopter work quite impossible.

In the afternoon of the following day the weather lifted somewhat. The orphans were located from the air and the helicopter was used to drive them towards a remote farm road where the ground crew could move in once they had been darted.

The orphans resisted, though, and ran towards a valley. How terrified they must have been by the loud, low helicopter trying to herd them where they did not want to go . . .

These were 'cull' orphans from the Kruger National Park. According to the Chambers English Dictionary, the word 'cull' means *pick out from a herd and kill for the good of the herd*. 'Cull' in the southern African conservation context, particularly with regard to elephant policy, means the extermination of entire family groups of elephants.

The only survivors of these mass slaughters would be calves of a specific height and age. After witnessing the destruction of their entire families, these young elephants would be captured for export into the international wildlife trade for zoos and circuses, or sold for introduction into other game reserves.

Brought to the Knysna Forest in 1994, the young Kruger orphans had just seen their entire kin group murdered. The herd would have become fearful on hearing the distant *phud, phud, phud* sound of the helicopter. We know that elephants are highly intelligent animals and after years of culling in the Kruger National Park, the elephant family knew that the sound of helicopters was associated with death.

Up until 1995, when a moratorium on the culling of elephants was introduced in the Kruger National Park, culls had taken place routinely and annually for more than two and a half decades.[4]

Even the non-targeted herds would have felt the terror during culling time. In the 1980s, it was discovered that elephants use infrasonic communication, sounds that travel long distances at frequencies well below the range of human hearing. As a result, all elephants within a radius of some 15 kilometres of where a cull was taking place would be aware of the trauma. In fact, to be brutally honest, it was far worse than that, but we simply did not know this at the time.

Recent research into elephant communication has revealed that they can hear one another over perhaps hundreds of kilometres through seismic waves travelling through the ground. Therefore, wherever mass killing of elephants takes place, entire populations are affected, creating far-reaching distress and trauma.

And on that day in July 1999, it was happening all over again in the minds of the Kruger orphans. *Phud, phud, phud*. The helicopter blades droned, slicing through the air, terrifying the orphans. Images of the massacre of their entire families must have flooded into their minds.

The helicopter closed in on the orphans and, terrified, they ran and ran. But before long, the helicopter was hovering directly above them. Suddenly one of the orphans pulled back, and as the helicopter

---

[4] Tragically for the elephants of South Africa, this moratorium was lifted by the Department of Environmental Affairs and Tourism in 2008. Culling is once again a 'management' option.

passed over her, she raised her trunk, appearing for all the world to be calling to her friend, telling her to turn back. Amazingly, this is what happened. The orphan being pursued by the helicopter turned and ran back to where her friend was standing, waiting.

Then they began running in another direction, but the helicopter also turned around and flew after them like a massive persistent bee. They now ran side by side, shoulder to shoulder, along the mountain slope. A dart was fired from the helicopter. A young elephant screamed. Then there was another thud. The orphans ran on, but both now had tranquillising darts hooked into the skin of their rumps.

Then they went down, and it was all over. The helicopter landed and while the ground crew got to work, the blades finally stopped turning.

Soon men were pushing one of the orphans into position to be moved. A forest guard, Wilfred Oraai, held the end of the elephant's trunk to protect it. Wilfred turned to look behind him at the shoving, grunting men. Then he looked, with concern, at the orphan's face. He turned his head to look at the tip of the elephant's trunk that he was gently holding in his hands. Wilfred's eyes mirrored something beyond concern, something much deeper, an enormous sadness. It looked as though Wilfred was holding the hand of the orphan, attempting to comfort and console her, but all the time Wilfred's own heart was bursting with sadness. He had grown to love these elephants. He had monitored their movements on foot from the day of their release, almost five years earlier.

As time passed, the orphans came to know their followers, and would even allow Wilfred and his colleague Karel to watch them from as close as 50 metres. At times, it seemed that the guards, the watchers, became the watched while the elephants moved closer, feeding slowly, their heads turning towards the men.

Now that the orphans had been captured, those wonderful days were over for ever. Wilfred tried in vain to keep back the tears. He felt as though his heart was breaking . . .

At the very moment that Wilfred was holding the orphan's trunk, a lone female elephant was listening. The Matriarch was standing somewhere to the southwest, on the very edge of the forest, occasionally raising her trunk. She had heard, and literally felt, the trauma of the orphans. The trauma had travelled through the air, and through the very ground on which she was standing. It had been everywhere.

The grand old lady of the forest stayed there, listening, as it grew dark.

She undoubtedly associated the orphans' trauma with the helicopter and with people, believing that the people were pursuing the orphans in order to kill them, particularly as she would never again pick up the orphans' infrasonic calls. No doubt she had felt a very deep sadness . . . a sadness like Wilfred's.

Some time after midnight, after the truck containing the orphans had made its way out of the foothills, the Matriarch finally moved away, a phantom elephant once more.

The Matriarch turned her back on humankind, no longer moving in what had for so long been her old haunts. Her great footsteps were now found only very occasionally on the road called Kom se Pad, which winds through the centre of the main forest.

In time, she simply disappeared. Vanished completely. Some of the forest people believed that she had died. And although it was not talked about openly, the forest people asked in hushed tones, 'Is this finally the end, the end of the elephants of Knysna? Where is the old lady . . .?'

As I began writing this book, I discovered to my astonishment what might have caused my troubled state that evening after the very first time I visited the Knysna forest. When I was checking some dates in a diary, I discovered that Fransje and I had been in the forest on the same afternoon that the capture team had sought out the orphans. Coincidence? Synchronicity? Had I somehow sensed the orphans' trauma, and reacted to it? I can offer no real explanation . . .

F I V E

The Elephantine Miracle

The hills were not so high, and had gentle slopes; sometimes their flanks
began to move. It was the elephants . . .
Romain Gary
The Roots of Heaven, 1959

In the year of the new millennium, the year after the Kruger calves
had been captured and taken away, an elephantine miracle took place.

On 7 September 2000, forest guard Wilfred Oraai, the man who had
tenderly held the trunk of the Kruger orphan, was patrolling on a
road near the Gouna portion of the forests when suddenly he saw it.
A large dark shape loomed amongst the fynbos and ferns beneath a
stand of burnt pine trees.

Wilfred paused, held his breath, and stared . . .

The dark shape moved. Wilfred breathed out, then pulled his small
pair of binoculars out of his pocket and focused on the shape. He then
saw an elephant's trunk suddenly rise up in the air, before snaking
down to explore the fynbos vegetation.

Wilfred's heart pounded when he noticed that this elephant's left tusk
was about forty centimetres in length. This was very meaningful. In
fact, it meant the world in terms of the Knysna elephants.

The Matriarch, then thought to be the last surviving Knysna elephant, had long ago snapped her left tusk, leaving only a tiny stump visible from the grey fold of her lip.

In contrast, this elephant clearly had a left tusk and therefore the elephant that Wilfred was watching was definitely not the Matriarch. This was a 'new' Knysna elephant, an elephant whose existence no one had known of.

Not until this day.

Excitedly Wilfred peered through his binoculars, noting that the elephant's head seemed more rounded than that of the Matriarch. It was a young bull!

It was as if this elephant had come out of nowhere, yet of course it must have been there all the time. Or had it? What else could explain its presence? This was not a case of natural recruitment. The closest elephant population, the fenced-in elephants of the Addo National Park, where every individual was known and accounted for, was hundreds of kilometres away to the east.

It was unbelievable to Wilfred. He had patrolled these forests for many years and, after the removal of his beloved orphans, had known of no other elephants other than the Matriarch.

Although Wilfred would not publicly say so at the time, he privately doubted whether she was even still alive. He had not found any sign of the Matriarch for at least a year now.

The word 'evidence' rang loudly in Wilfred's mind. He knew that he had to document, to photograph, this elephant with a left tusk, to prove its existence. He pulled a small camera from his rucksack, checked the direction of the wind, and then silently moved towards the elephant.

He took the first photograph from about fifty metres away, capturing the elephant with its trunk raised. But once he had taken the photograph, Wilfred thought that the left tusk, the all-important vital evidence, had been obscured by vegetation as the shutter clicked. He would have to creep closer to the elephant to attempt a clear photograph of the left tusk.

He moved in until he was only thirty metres from where the elephant was feeding and then pulled himself up into one of the burnt pines. Elevated, and looking down on the elephant, Wilfred now had a clear view. He took a second, third and fourth photograph of the elephant below him. Then he simply watched and marvelled.

After patrolling the forest for more than six years, almost five of them spent searching for and monitoring the Kruger orphans, Wilfred was looking at an elephant he had never seen before. There, up in the tree, he shook his head and wondered where on earth this elephant had come from. Where had it been all those months and years that he and Karel had patrolled, covering thousands of kilometres through forest, fynbos and plantations? This elephant had simply appeared that day as if in a dream.

Later the elephant began moving away to the west, allowing Wilfred to climb down the tree and follow cautiously for a while. He snapped a final photograph as the elephant moved down the steep Knysna gorge, and it was this photograph that was later to reveal a curious thing. There appeared to be pink patches on top of the elephant's head, on the nape of its neck, and on the top of its wide ears. Could this perhaps be partial albinism? In the Far East exceptionally rare albino elephants are regarded as very holy beings.

Wilfred left the elephant and made his way up the gorge to the road in the burnt pine plantation, where he turned on his two-way radio to report his remarkable sighting to forester Len du Plessis. The conversation that ensued was a very excited one.

News of Wilfred's sighting and the photographs of the Young Bull astonished everyone who heard the story or read about it in the newspapers. International news reports of the Young Bull appeared. These were, after all, the most endangered elephants in the world.

Locally, people wondered how the Young Bull, estimated from the photographs to be about sixteen to eighteen years old, could have gone undetected for so many years and why there had been only this single sighting in the past decade and a half. Other questions were raised. Who was the Young Bull's mother and, indeed, who was his father?

The appearance of the Young Bull meant that prior to the female Kruger orphans being removed the year before, there had been a small but viable breeding nucleus of elephants all along. By declaring the Matriarch the last Knysna elephant, and then by removing the Kruger orphans from their adopted home, the authorities had committed an ecological bungle.

S I X

Beginnings

It was not just because of its size that the elephant intrigued me so much. Its strength and dignity, its silent movement and sudden trumpeting fury, its sociable life in the herd, the humour of its young, the threatening beauty of its tusks, the delicate twist and touch of its trunk and the intelligent look in its wise old eye if I managed to get close to it, all these enthralled me.
George Adamson
My Pride and Joy, 1986

Early in 2001, having completed and promoted a new book,[5] Fransje and I made the decision to move to the southern Cape where I would embark upon an independent and low-key study of the Knysna elephants. This was about six months after Wilfred had sighted the Young Bull.

I felt very strongly that this was something that I just had to do. So, in May 2001 we settled into a wooden house on a high ridge that overlooked the Knysna lagoon and the Indian Ocean to the south. Beyond the northern side of the ridge were the forests of Knysna. Rising from the central forests is the Jonkersberg Mountain, behind which, way in the distance, beyond the high veiling haze, are the brooding peaks of the Outeniqua Mountain range. With ocean and lakes, lagoons, forests and mountains, I think this must be one of the most beautiful places in the world.

---

[5] *To Walk with Lions,* Rider Books, 2001.

The field environs in which I would be spending hundreds of hours in the years ahead were very different to the conditions I had worked in before. In both Southern Africa and East Africa I had lived in very hot and dry wild lands where one could walk for an entire day, and yet the horizon would appear unchanged. One feels very small in a place where the horizon remains still and unmoving.

Here in Knysna, when I am in the forest there is simply no horizon at all. But this makes one feel equally small. In the forests I am tightly surrounded by thousands of trees set in hundreds of square kilometres of land. As you walk in these forests, you feel as if you are walking beneath a vast army of venerable great green giants. Should you venture off the trail, the trees are so close together that they seem almost to squeeze you. The view skywards is blocked by the jigsaw puzzle of forest canopy.

It is an enchanted place. These great forest trees, I am sure, have souls. Because they are so big, so unmoving, one would expect them to be like monuments, cold and still. But they are not. The forest trees pulsate with an invisible life and energy, and each tree is very much an individual. Each has its unique sense of presence. In the forests, I am amongst crowds of individual beings.

The forest environment was entirely new to me, and I was like a child to the place; I had so much to learn from everything around me. In other areas where I had worked, I had already known my immediate surroundings for many years.

In the Tuli bushlands, for example, I knew the lie of the land. I knew its secret valleys, wide plains and dense riverine bush. I knew the extremities of the climate, the scorching hot days, followed by violent, flooding rains. The animals of that place, from squirrels to impala to lions and elephants – I had known them for many years. I knew the ground's scarred face, marked by the feet and hooves of the wild ones who lived there.

But when I first came to the Knysna forests and the mountains I had no experience of the ways of the place, apart from what I had read about the area. I knew from the outset that this would be a very challenging project, and that I would have to learn for myself. I had no mentors or teachers apart from the forest and the mountains themselves. I was going to leave behind most of my knowledge of the dry bushlands, and now had to learn afresh in this strange, magical place.

I was to work in the field totally alone, which in part had been a conscious decision. I wanted to enter the forest and to climb the mountainsides unobtrusively and unhindered, stepping quietly as I began to build up information on the Knysna elephants. For as long as possible, I wanted to gently deflect any attention from what I was doing. The reason for this was because I knew that controversy and human politics have hung over the invisible backs of the Knysna elephants for a great many years. To learn as much as I could about the secret elephants, for the greater part of the project I had to be secretive like the elephants themselves.

My work was largely self-funded. The project drained my modest savings, but for almost six years, I was to have almost total independence. And that was priceless.

Strangely, I felt only a little foreboding setting out alone into unknown places in those early days. I think this was because I embraced the forest's quietness completely.

The general baseline objectives of the elephant study were the following:
- To try to establish how many Knysna elephants remained
- To establish the extent of the range of the elephants
- To establish which habitats the elephants used within that range
- To establish the diet of the Knysna elephants

Elephants are water-dependent animals, and normally they drink on a daily basis. I knew at the outset of the study that if I could find a favoured drinking place of the Knysna elephants, I would be closer to unlocking what was going on in the lives of this tiny, relic population.

Also, knowing that, at the most, the forest guards sighted Knysna elephants only once or twice a year, I knew that it was likely that I'd never even see an elephant. Instead, I would be learning about them from signs they left behind on their wanderings – their droppings, their tracks, and feeding signs such as strewn branches, leaves and other disturbed vegetation.

With time and patience one can learn a lot about an animal one cannot see. However, one has to become something of an animal detective. Analysis of droppings, for example, would tell me what the elephants were eating. An elephant eats up to one hundred and fifty kilograms of vegetation each day, and in turn deposits about one hundred kilograms of droppings in the same amount of time. Because they digest only about 40 per cent of what they eat, examination of elephant droppings would tell me not only *what* they ate, but also *where* they had been feeding.

Trees and plants live in specific communities. They all have their niches, and so finding out what the elephants ate would also indicate what habitat they had been feeding in. Finding strewn vegetation where they had been feeding, and recording the plant species they fed upon, would also contribute to building up a picture about the elephants' diet.

Interestingly, it has been found that grass generally makes up about 70 per cent of the diet of savannah elephants in the wet season, with larger proportions of browse, the twigs, leaves, bark etc of the trees, contributing to their diets as the dry season progresses. What picture would emerge here of savannah elephants inhabiting a landscape where there is very little grass? How had these elephants adapted to the lack of what is normally their principal diet in the wet season?

Generally, savannah elephants inhabit predictable home ranges in the dry season, but migrate over large areas in the wet season. In direct contrast to the climate of most of southern Africa, this portion of the southern Cape receives rainfall that is distributed fairly evenly throughout the year. How does this influence the Knysna elephants' movements? These were just some of many complex questions to be unlocked in the early days.

In the months ahead, through my study of the diet of the Knysna elephants, I was to uncover startling and previously unknown information about them. My research revealed that the elephants might even hold knowledge of medicine . . .

A great many plants around the world are named after animals which have appeared to use them for medicinal purposes. For example, the Navajo Native American people, having observed bears digging up and using the roots of the *Ligusticum* plants so frequently with apparent benefits, had named the plant 'bear medicine'. In the forests of Knysna, I discovered that the elephants were using something so frequently that it could be referred to as 'elephant medicine'.

Through extensive research over many years, we have learnt more about elephants than perhaps any other large, wild living mammal. Yet at the same time, we have only just begun to comprehend their complex lives and ways. My discovery was to underline the fact that we have so much more to learn about elephants.

What I discovered, in short, was that it seemed that the Knysna elephants were self-medicating to ensure their survival. I found that they were routinely eating something known in ancient Chinese traditional medicine as 'The Herb of Longevity'. It had never before been known that elephants eat this 'herb'.

But that would happen much later on. First, I must tell of my early forays into the forests, and of the very first signs I found of the mysterious Knysna elephants.

S E V E N

Into the Forest

I set out to walk the forests of Knysna for the very first time on a bright morning in May 2001. I chose a fifteen-kilometre trail through dense forest, just south of the Diepwalle forest station. The reason I chose this particular area was because that portion of the forest was part of the known range of the Matriarch.

In retrospect, I think I was also drawn to that area, almost subconsciously, because it was the place where the pendulum had indicated the position of the missing helicopter.

Before setting off on the trail, I struck up a very interesting conversation with an elderly man who managed the indigenous nursery at the forest station. To learn about the Knysna elephants I knew that it was important to speak to the forest people because this was their home as much as it was the elephants' home.

I learnt from the man that he had been with the forestry department for his entire adult life. The following year, he told me, he was due to retire after some thirty-five years of service. He was typical of many of the forest people, such as the forest guards, with whom I would speak in the weeks and months ahead. They are quietly spoken, polite, and very attuned to the forest.

I believe that one becomes imbued, in a sense, with the environment in which one lives, by the 'personality' of that environment. And living and working within the forest, I think one cannot help but be humbled by its almost overwhelming 'personality'.

For example, when I asked the nurseryman where he would retire to the following year, he looked a little surprised before answering, 'Oh, I won't be going anywhere. This is my place. I will continue to stay here at the "Bosdorp" (bush village) at Diepwalle.' He would remain in the forest. It was, simply, his home and where he belonged.

As we chatted, I asked him about the Young Bull, the mysterious 'new' Knysna elephant that had been sighted and photographed by the forest guard Wilfred Oraai a few months earlier.

'That's right, that's right,' he said cheerfully. 'The Young Bull stays over in the western side, in the Gouna part of the forests.'

Then, with a touch of pride, he recounted what transpired after Wilfred saw the elephant.

'Man, at first, we forest people could not believe it. It was great. Another Knysna elephant! And that young man Wilfred, he was very brave and clever. He even managed to snap some photos of the elephant. That was the solid evidence,' he emphasised.

'With that evidence,' he continued, 'the newspapers and the radio told the story. Even television people came here to the forest to make a film about how Wilfred found the Young Bull. The whole community here at Diepwalle was very proud of Wilfred. He had done a very good job finding this new elephant.'

I then asked him the current situation about the Young Bull, and whether the elephant had been seen again recently.

'The Young Bull has not been sighted again, but Wilfred, with his colleague, Karel Maswatie, they follow its spoor at times and continue to look for it,' he replied.

I asked him how it could be that the Young Bull had been here for almost two decades, yet had only recently been sighted for the very first time. The elderly man paused for a second, then smiled indulgently at me, the obvious newcomer to the forest.

'The forests are very big,' he explained. 'And though elephants are huge, the forests make them small in comparison. They are like a few lonely fleas on the back of a big furry dog.' He chuckled.

'Let me put it this way,' he continued. 'It is like the whales and the ocean here. Whales are massive animals and can be as long as fifteen elephants standing in a row. Just imagine that! Fifteen elephants in a row! Now, if you go to the Kranshoek cliffs overlooking the ocean any time between the months of June and November, the season of the whales, you might be lucky enough to see one. But let me ask you this. How will the whale look to you in the sea?'

I was beginning to understand the analogy he was drawing.

I replied, 'It would look small, relative to the size of the ocean.'

'Exactly, exactly,' the man said, nodding his head. 'And so it is with the elephants here in the forests. The forests are big and so, as if like magic, they make the elephants small. The trees are the true giants here, not the elephants.'

He waved his hand over the forest below us and said, 'This place is like an ocean, and the elephants are like whales here. But,' he said after a pause, 'you cannot go to a high place here and expect to see elephants because, unlike the surface of the sea, the giant trees, of course, they cover this place! There is a saying about trying to find a needle in a haystack, yes?'

I nodded.

'Well, here to find an elephant is like looking for a needle that can move about, this way and that, in a massive haystack, the forest. And so it is with the Young Bull, he is like a moving needle. That is why he was never seen before. And that is why it was so great, so fantastic, that Wilfred managed not only to see the new elephant, but to have photographed it as well.'

I then asked him whether the Matriarch had been seen recently, but at the mention of her name, the man's cheerful manner changed abruptly. He went silent and did not answer me for a minute or so. Then, he looked out south across the forests and muttered quietly, almost to himself, 'Maybe she is still out there somewhere . . .'

The transformation in the man's mood was dramatic. I had obviously touched on a very sensitive subject and I knew that I, the newcomer here, should not continue to ask about the Matriarch. But his answer had shocked me.

Could the Matriarch have died?

I thanked the man for his time, and said that I would very much like to talk to him again sometime about his years in the forest.

He looked at me with a small lopsided smile, and said, 'Yes, we can talk again sometime.'

And with that, he turned and walked slowly back to attend to his nursery.

I then set off on the forest trail. The nurseryman's reaction to my mentioning the Matriarch had been almost like an expression of deeply felt grief. The old man would have known of the presence of the Matriarch for his entire working life in the forest, and in a sense he and the elderly elephant were bonded together by those long years. Her apparent disappearance had obviously affected him deeply.

The 'official' status of the Matriarch was that she was still alive. A few days earlier I had gone to the forestry department's head office in town, and had asked the Information Officer what was the official number of remaining Knysna elephants. The answer had been: 'Two, the Matriarch and the Young Bull.'

But on that first day in the forest I had just heard that this might not be the case . . .

In 1994 a forester, Johan Huisamen, came across the Matriarch as she emerged from a forest path. Johan had a camera with him, and took a remarkable photograph of her. This photograph has since been published in books, magazines and newspapers, locally and internationally. The image is also used for a forestry department postcard. On the back of the postcard it states, rather depressingly: 'The Last Remaining Knysna Elephant'.

The photograph shows the Matriarch, with sunlight streaking down on her head, surrounded by a mosaic of green vegetation. Her right tusk can be clearly seen, jutting out prominently. Her left tusk, though, had snapped off long ago and in the photograph only a few inches of ivory can be seen beneath the grey hide of her lip. One senses weariness exuding from her. Her trunk lies straight down in front of her. The tip of the trunk is touching the ground. In the photograph, her body is tilting slightly to one side, as though she was about to turn away slowly when she was captured on film.

This photograph, this image of the old lady, had become indelibly etched into my mind for several months before Fransje and I moved down to Knysna to begin the project. I stared at the photograph for ages, studying it to see what else it could reveal of this elusive, lone elephant. With his photograph Johan had captured a living, breathing legend. He had unlocked an ageless mystery. Through that photograph, the Matriarch became almost tangible to me. She lived and, somehow, she seemed timeless.

As I began to walk along the trail, many questions flooded my mind. What if the Matriarch had died? Would that mean that the Young Bull was the very last Knysna elephant? Yet, perhaps she was not dead, but had moved away from her old haunts? Was I reading too much into the nurseryman's reaction?

And so it was with mixed emotions that I walked away into the forest for the very first time.

I was surprised by the quietness of the forest and wondered whether it was always like that. Silence hung over the place like a cloak. Even birdcalls were few. The stillness was so overwhelming that I caught myself leaping around quickly when I heard a shuffling of leaves. It was only an olive thrush scratching amongst the leaf litter, searching for insects. But I was startled again in the quietness when the bird, now alarmed by my presence, cried loudly and flew up on to a branch.

I chuckled nervously to myself, thinking what a ridiculous thing it was to be startled by a thrush. I knew that in reality this was just the beginning of becoming accustomed to an entirely new wild environment. And in the weeks and months ahead I did, indeed, become used to the forest's ways and idiosyncrasies.

For example, in time I learnt that different trees 'speak' with different voices. Whenever there was a general breeze in the air, the leaves of the forest trees would almost gurgle softly in unison. The most 'talkative' trees, I learnt, were the eucalyptus, the gums in the plantation areas. Even the slightest breeze would make the air suddenly shiver anxiously with an almost paranoid shaking of their leaves. And the older gums – well, they really caught me out in the early days with their sudden, loud, eerie creaking sounds. I froze upon hearing these sounds and peered around anxiously. But, again, in time I grew used to the sighs and groans of the old trees.

On the trail that day, I came across different signs of the forest animals that lived there. I frequently saw the spoor of bushpig, and the delicate hoof prints of bushbuck, a beautiful medium-sized antelope. I also came across the pugmarks of a leopard. I was heartened to see for myself that these big cats still lived in the forests. The footprints indicated that it was a young leopard, perhaps only recently having left its mother to establish a territory of its own.

But of elephants there was absolutely no sign at all. Not even the oldest of droppings, or the vaguest evidence of feeding. Yet this was part of the known range of the Matriarch . . . I began to feel a slight uneasiness as I carried on walking.

I might have been in an environment new to me, but my tracking eyes were still keen. I had found signs of bushbuck, bushpig and leopard. As the nurseryman had explained, yes, the elephants themselves were extremely elusive, but despite this they would leave evidence of feeding, and of course droppings, behind them on their lonely wanderings. And so I concluded that, for whatever reason, the elephants had not visited the area for many weeks.

Had I come to this place too late? Was the Matriarch no longer alive?

With no answer to that question, I continued on the trail, heading back towards the Diepwalle forest station.

As I walked the last few kilometres along an old forest road known as Petrus Brand Pad, I suddenly began to feel very ill at ease. Then I remembered. Petrus Brand Pad, south of Diepwalle. This was the place that the pendulum had indicated the helicopter might have crashed in the forest back in 1999. Looking around at the dense vegetation on both sides of the forest road, I shivered and began to walk faster.

In the months, even years ahead, I hardly ever returned to that place on Petrus Brand Pad.

The following day I set out on a trail in the western part of the main forest in the vicinity of the Gouna forest station. It was in this area, the nurseryman had told me, that the Young Bull roamed at times. The path narrowed as I descended into a deep, cold gorge. At the bottom I crossed a small gurgling stream before I climbed up the valley. It was difficult to imagine elephants willingly traversing through gorges like this one. Apart from the steep terrain, it was a dark, damp, shadowy place.

As I reached the top of the gorge, I suddenly saw the movement of an animal. I froze. Then I saw two dark shapes. I stepped forward quietly. In a rare patch of forest clearing, I saw two male bushbuck. Both had beautifully curved horns, and they continued peacefully browsing, totally unaware of my presence. I crouched down and stalked forward until finally I was no more than 15 metres away from them. I noticed that the forest had become almost totally silent. Not just quiet, but almost as if everything around me was holding its breath. Not a leaf stirred. There was a strange tension that I had never before experienced in the wilds. Though enthralled to be watching the bushbuck at such close quarters, part of me began to feel uneasy in the almost echoing silence.

Suddenly, a very loud dog-like bark erupted in the air and in quick succession another two more explosions of sound erupted. The bushbuck had sensed my presence and had barked in alarm before crashing heavily through the forest. As they did, the trees around me vibrated, together with a loud unison of urgent birdcalls and the sounds of insects. The sounds seemed to be coming from everywhere. It was as if the forest inhabitants were venting some kind of collective alarm.

Danger! Danger! the forest screamed.

My unusual sense of unease – it was almost guilt – increased tenfold. I quickly moved away, wishing to create some distance from the almost scornful sounds. I even muttered soft apologies as I walked off. This new wild place was definitely unlike anywhere I had been before.

The forest, its plant life, wild animals, birds, insects and everything else was like a single living, breathing entity. A sentient entity, almost . . .

I found no signs or evidence whatsoever of elephants that day.

Was the Matriarch no longer alive? Where was the Young Bull?

E I G H T

Signs of the Elephants

One day, during the first month of the project, I happened to overhear a conversation between two men in the Knysna library. The topic of the conversation was the Knysna elephants. One man was, like me, clearly a newcomer to the area, while the other, an older man, apparently had lived there for years.

'Back in the 1970s, admittedly, yes, the Knysna elephants were still around then,' the older man said knowledgeably, 'but they have all died out since. It was inevitable anyway. Couldn't be helped. In the end, there was just the one poor old female wandering around on her own. But there hasn't been any sign of her for a good couple of years.'

The younger man nodded and I thought, but what about the Young Bull photographed by the forest guard Wilfred, then?

'Some of the locals, though,' the older man continued with a wry chuckle, 'they like to keep the story of the elephants going, good for tourism, and this town depends on tourism. Every once in a while somebody will claim to have seen an elephant, or droppings or footprints. Then it might get into the local rags. Funny thing is, these so-called sightings usually take place in the peak tourism times. It is a great story for the tourists to go home with. You know,' he stated dramatically, ' "Legendary Knysna elephant sighted," and all that. Bit of a sad joke, really.'

'So,' the younger man asked, slightly aghast, 'so you're saying that there are no more elephants at all in the forests. That they're all dead now?'

'Dead as the dodo. Stuff of myth and legend now, I'm afraid,' the older man responded. 'Lives on only in stories, a bit like the myth of the Loch Ness monster.'

I walked away with the books I had chosen, not wanting to hear any more.

Those very early days in the forest were perplexing times. During the first forays, I did not find any evidence that elephants existed. Not the slightest trace.

With hindsight, I know that the forest and the elephants had simply been yielding their secrets very reluctantly. It would take a lot of tenacity and perseverance to obtain even a glimpse into the secret world of the Knysna elephants. It was for this reason that so little was known about them. When I first set out to undertake my study, no one had any real insight into the lives of the present-day Knysna elephants, apart from the forest guards. Because of the local conditions, it had not been possible to study the elephants by any conventional methods such as aerial census or radio tracking.

I realised that the Knysna elephants were in all likelihood among the most difficult animals to study anywhere in the world.

One morning during the first month I was on Kom se Pad, the old woodcutters' road that winds through the main forest, when I found two separate piles of elephant droppings. The man in the library was wrong. Elephants certainly did still exist.

The size of the balls of dung in both piles indicated that they were from young elephants. In addition, the balls of dung in one pile were distinctly smaller than those in the other pile, indicating the existence of two young Knysna elephants.

As I examined the contents of the droppings, I noticed that the vegetation content had been well ground down, which again indicated that these were young elephants, and not the Matriarch. At an estimated age of fifty-four, the Matriarch's last set of molars would have worn down, so she would not be chewing food as thoroughly as younger elephants. During an elephant's lifetime, which is just a little shorter than a human one, they have six sets of molars. As one set gradually wears down, a new set moves forward to take the place of the old ones. Usually the sixth and final set is in use by the time an elephant reaches the age of about forty.

If I was right, then what I had deduced from the first two piles of droppings I had found would be fairly significant. There was now evidence that, at the very least, two young Knysna elephants existed.

The following day I set off on a forest trail that led through the central forest, close to where I had found the first droppings. As I walked that morning, I first 'felt', and then later saw the presence of elephants. The trail, I was soon to realise, was part of the oldest roads in Africa, the elephant pathways. These pathways exist all over the continent, and I believe they possess a certain powerful energy, a form of magnetism perhaps, after being utilised by countless elephants over hundreds of years.

It was interesting to notice that unlike the other trails I had followed so far, it was only here that I felt the energy of an elephant pathway. So perhaps it was not surprising that I soon found physical evidence of elephants on this particular trail.

I noticed flecks of earth on the bark of a tree beside the pathway, and reached up to touch the mud. It was clear to see that this had been left behind after an elephant had brushed alongside the tree. Wrinkled etched skin had touched the equally wrinkled and etched skin of the tree.

Touching the muddied bark was almost like touching the elephant itself. Despite having found the droppings the previous day, it was here, when touching the bark that the elephant had brushed against, that these animals became real to me. When I touched that tree, the Knysna elephants stepped out of the realms of rumour and old stories.

The elephant pathway led me down to the Gouna River, a river that winds along from its place of birth, the catchment area up in the mountains to the north, and snakes through the main part of the forest. Just as I was about to step from one small boulder to the next in order to cross the river, I saw the footprint of a young elephant embedded in grass and mud right on the water line on the southern bank. I felt the imprint delicately with my fingers. As I touched it, it was once again almost like touching the elephant itself.

The spoor seemed fairly fresh. At this place, only a day or so ago, a young Knysna elephant had crossed the Gouna River. The size of the footprint indicated that this elephant was probably a teenager. The Young Bull, perhaps.

I stepped over the boulders and crossed the river. In front of me was a steep, slimy incline of mud and rocks. Surely, I thought, the elephant had not climbed up here.

But it had. As I scrambled up the narrow, wet path, I again saw the elephant's footprints. Remarkably, with its great feet squishing in mud and upon greasy wet rock, the elephant had climbed the steep fifteen-metre high riverbank before pulling itself up on to the more level area of forest at the top.

When I reached the lip of the embankment, I looked down at the pathway, trying to imagine the elephant as it made its way up from the river over the wet rocks and sinking mud. What a sight that must have been.

Even though it was difficult to imagine an elephant moving up such terrain, I knew that elephants were masters at crossing difficult ground. Hannibal, after all, during the campaign against the Romans, had led an army of thirty-seven elephants through the Alps. The elephants proved to be remarkable climbers, with an excellent head for heights.

I walked on, following the faint tracks of the young elephant before entering a maze of tall forest tree ferns, plants with long, soft out-stretched fronds that almost plead to be touched and caressed. There among the forest tree ferns, I came across the day-old droppings of the young elephant. As I was about to crouch down to examine my find, I noticed a buckled and scarred metal sign on the ground nearby. It was a trail marker that would have been attached to a tree to guide hikers through this portion of the forest.

I turned the sign over and marvelled. The trail was appropriately known as the 'Elephant Walk', and the yellow metal sign depicted an image of an elephant. Now, a live version of that image had tusked the sign from the tree before proceeding to mangle it.

The young elephant had continued onwards, crossing Kom se Pad, the track where I had found the old droppings the day before. From the faint signs I found that morning, the elephant had then headed up towards the mountains beyond the forest. This alone was of interest, as it was thought at the time that the elephants were confined to the forest.

The following day I set out on a trail in the northerly direction that the young elephant had taken. I had brought a powerful amplified microphone and headphones to help me pick up any further clues. As elephants spend almost 70 per cent of their time feeding, I felt it might even be possible to locate them by sound.

After venturing deep into the forest for about an hour, I decided to test my sound equipment. I put the headphones on and switched on the amplified microphone, listening to the forest sounds for a minute or so.

Suddenly harsh loud sawing sounds slammed into my ears. *Leopard!* I tore the headphones off, hearing the territorial call of a leopard coming some 200 metres from where I was standing. Then, rather ominously, the calls stopped.

I knew that leopards called as they walked, so I quickly backed away up the path. Minutes later I heard the calls again. This time they were even louder, coming from a spot close to where I had been standing just minutes before. Never before, nor since, have I heard leopards calling during daylight hours, and I wondered if this one might have been a female in oestrus.

It was thrilling to have heard the leopard. The footprints and other signs of leopard that I came across during my wanderings in the months ahead indicated that these magnificent big cats had made something of a comeback in and around the vicinity of the Knysna forests. Thirty years earlier their numbers were so low that they were regarded as very rare indeed.

I continued onwards in search of signs of the young elephant and soon came across elephant footprints on a muddy section of the path. The tracks looked similar in size to those I had found on the banks of the Gouna River the day before.

Further along I found a pile of elephant droppings, and nearby branches were strewn where clearly the elephant had been feeding. The footprints and the feeding signs were an indication that the elephant had continued northwards towards the mountains. As I was about to continue on its tracks, I suddenly saw another metal sign on the ground. I reached down and turned it over. 'Elephant Walk', it read, just like the hiking route marker I had found the day before. This one was equally bent and mangled. This elephant definitely had a penchant for pulling down the hiking trail markers, and I wondered why.

I continued on my way, now climbing increasingly into the high forest on the southern side of the Jonkersberg Mountain. According to my map, I knew that soon I would reach the edge of the forest, and would come out into fynbos country, close to the top of the mountain.

I finally emerged from the forest and blinked as the dazzling sunlight hit my eyes. I looked around me and felt as though I was on top of the world. Below me, the forest lay spread out like an enormous dark green blanket, and beyond was the Indian Ocean. To the north lay the peaks and valleys of the Outeniqua Mountains, looking like the jagged back of some mighty dragon that had been frozen in time.

Then, on the trail ahead of me, I saw the deeply embedded footprints of an elephant. What a sight it must be to see a Knysna elephant out in the open, walking on top of the mountain with the dark, damp forests below, and the crisp blue sky all around.

Nearby I also found some older footprints, and further on some more that were larger than the others. From the signs and evidence I had found the Knysna elephants, contrary to previous belief, were not at all restricted to the forests.

That evening as I rested my weary body and prepared to sleep, I visualised the elephants walking on the top of that mountain, high above the forest.

PART TWO

N I N E

Brother Elephant

They (the white hunters) *came from the Cape itself and from abroad, they killed not from need but for pleasure, and not in ones or twos but in huge numbers; they hunted . . . in the last century and killed a multitude of animals . . . The great company of wild animals has gone . . .*
Eve Palmer
The Plains of Camdeboo, 1966

It was both remarkable and wonderful to have seen actual evidence of the present-day Knysna elephants. Given the changes, and impacts of time, it was miraculous that elephants still existed where the land had been colonised by the white settlers three hundred years ago. Indeed it was this southern-most portion of the country that had first felt the dramatic brunt of the colonist's exploitative use of wildlife.

Other animal species such as lion, black rhinoceros, wild dog, brown hyena, reedbuck, red hartebeest, mountain zebra, hippopotamus, eland, buffalo, springbok, and even the little black-backed jackal had all long ago been eradicated from the very same land on which I was following the trail of the elephants in 2001.

Lions had been wiped out as early as 1775. Buffalo once roamed here in their thousands. The very last one was shot dead in 1883. Two animal species, the blue buck and the quagga, a close relative of the plains zebra, were eradicated. The last quagga died in a zoo in

Amsterdam in 1883, only seventy-two years after first being seen and recorded by the white man.

Even the 'first people' of this southern part of Africa, the San, were commonly hunted down and killed with impunity by the white settlers. Knowing that they engaged in this appalling practice, one can only imagine on what scale the wildlife was slaughtered by the settlers. Millions of animals died. The arrival of the settlers was like the coming of a great plague to this place.

Thus the level of wildlife extermination since the arrival of the colonists, together with the vast changes that have taken place across the landscape in the following years, make it even more incredible that any Knysna elephants survived into the twentieth century, let alone into the new millennium.

During the 1880s it was thought that there were approximately 400 to 600 of these elephants left. In 1994 it was stated that only one remained, the Matriarch. So when I found those footprints on the pathway high on top of the Jonkersberg Mountain, it was as if I had been transported back into a different time and space, a time before the arrival of the settlers.

Prior to the arrival of the settlers, herds of elephants roamed the coastal plains, travelling on their ancient pathways from feeding place to feeding place.

At night, lions called. And those great guttural sounds were followed by the piercing cries of the jackals, wily little carnivores whose almond-shaped eyes are quick to monitor the movements of lion prides. Late in the night, great sawing sounds cut ominously through the air. These were the calls of the leopard that lived on the slopes of the hills and in the deep kloofs along the Knysna River.

Then, at daybreak, the first people of this land, the San, emerged from their grassy shelters. The San people, hunter-gatherers, lived by hunting small and medium-sized mammals, by fishing, and by collecting roots, bulbs, seeds and corms of a host of plant species.

These people trod lightly upon the earth, believing that humans were animals in a previous existence, and were therefore related to the animals.

It appears that the elephant was a very important being to the San of the southern Cape. It was as if there was a deep spiritual bond between the people and the elephants. This is demonstrated, for example, in the San rock art of the region.

There are approximately 15 000 known rock art sites in the country, while the actual number that exists is probably double this. There are more rock paintings in the Cape than in any other part of Southern Africa and it is here where the San most often depicted the elephant in their art. In fact, the elephant has been represented overwhelmingly more often here than anywhere else. It is entirely possible that the San of the southern Cape saw the elephant as a 'power' animal, an animal that was associated with the bringing of rain.

San rock paintings are not crude depictions of traditional hunting scenes, as the colonists believed. They are in fact highly complex illustrations of mystical visions that were experienced by San shamans during 'trances', or altered states of consciousness. Trance state, achieved by dancing, singing and rhythmic clapping, was entered into so that the shamans could perform their duties and functions. They could continue uninterrupted for as long as three to four days. During the trance state, the shaman could transform into, or connect with animals, drawing on their power. In the final stages of this ritual the shaman became part of the hallucinatory 'other' spirit world.

These experiences of spiritual journeys and travels would later be depicted through complex art on rock faces. One researcher evocatively described San rock art as the 'fragments of the dance'.

Seeing the elephant as a rain animal, a being so important to their religious beliefs, it is unlikely that the original San in these parts would have harmed the elephant in any way. Instead, it is more likely that the elephant would have been a powerful totem animal for them. Totemism, the veneration of a sacred animal, is found in the belief systems of many cultures in Africa. Totem animals are sacred and must never be harmed or interfered with in any way.

Traditionally, African people regarded the elephant with very deep reverence. So often over the years African people have said to me, 'elephants are just like people'. The San of the southern Cape would have had an intimate understanding of the ways of elephants, their strong sense of family, their grief when a family member dies, and their love of their offspring. Many of these traits were also reflected in the San. They saw themselves in elephants. They revered the elephant because of a complex of values associated with family life and society. Children are of particular delight to San people, and they are very indulgent towards them. Elephants are the same.

It has been recorded that the last surviving San clans today in northern Namibia still regard the elephant as kin. They told a researcher that: 'We, of course, do not eat elephant. They are like a person . . . The female elephant has two breasts and they are on her chest just like a woman's.'

The parallels between elephants and the first people of the southern Cape would have been reflected in the plant foods utilised by both, and perhaps also in their knowledge of medicine. The original San of the southern Cape kept no livestock, nor did they undertake any form of agriculture. They were as much a part of the land as any of the other life of the sea, beaches, lakes, forest and mountains. On the ancient pathways of the elephants they would gather their foods, such as *Watsonia* corms, roots, bulbs and seeds. They would have waded in still waterways where elephants drank to collect the freshly opened flowers of water lilies, or *waterblommetjies*, as they are known today.

While gathering food, tonics and medicines would also be collected if needed. Today, some four thousand species of plants are known to be used for medicinal purposes in Southern Africa. What we know of the medicinal use of these species is usually ancient San knowledge handed down over the ages. The veld was their pharmacy.

What is not commonly known about the original San of the southern

Cape is that their lives went into some upheaval prior to the arrival of the white settlers. About one thousand years ago Khoikhoi herders brought cattle and sheep to the region and settled there. It is thought that they had moved southwards from what is today the northern part of Botswana.

The Khoikhoi were aboriginal people like the San (both being 'click speaking' people) but whose lifestyle had changed with the acquisition of livestock – first sheep and later cattle. The coming of the herders with their livestock impacted dramatically on the lives of the San. Before this, they and they alone were the nomads who roamed the southern Cape. The arrival of the Khoikhoi and their livestock altered the world view of the San, and impinged on the natural resources that they had not needed to share before. This new development created conflict between the San and the Khoikhoi. The San would steal livestock from the Khoikhoi and inevitable revenge would take place.

Over time, some of the San were absorbed by the Khoikhoi, and the opposite would have occurred when the Khoikhoi lost their livestock as a result of drought or disease. Such would have been the twists of fate over hundreds of years.

But the arrival of the Khoikhoi and their herds did not impact much on the elephants of the southern Cape. Like the San, ivory had no commercial value to the Khoikhoi. But this situation was shattered with the arrival of the early Dutch settlers and all those who came in their wake.

The San, the Khoikhoi and the elephants were all to share dark destinies. The lives of the people, the elephants and the other animals, and the land itself, was about to be changed for ever.

TEN

Mingled Destinies

Early in the project I had recognised the almost parallel lives, as well as the almost parallel fates, of the original San people and the elephants of the southern Cape. My knowledge of the definite existence of a few remaining Knysna elephants often made me ponder on the fate of the original San who had once shared this land with the elephants.

Somehow the elephants had managed to survive into the new millennium, but it seemed that the original San and their traditional way of life was lost early on with the settling of the land by the colonists. How had a tiny population of elephants survived, yet the original San and their way of life had seemingly vanished? Yes, the San survive today in the blood of the people of the southern Cape, but the way of life of a people who existed there for thousands of years appeared to have succumbed very quickly.

As I trekked through the forest and the mountains in those early days, I often wondered whether the last elephants had found refuge from the white man in the dense Knysna forests and lonely places in the mountain fynbos (places where, even today, people rarely venture), and whether some of the original San could have done likewise? Could a 'lost' people have survived into comparatively recent times in the same places I was seeking evidence of the last elephants?

To examine this question I had to look back at the impact of the arrival of the white settlers on the lives of the San, the Khoikhoi, and the elephants of the southern Cape.

The San and the Khoikhoi knew of the existence of people from other lands long before the arrival of Jan van Riebeeck and his founding of a supply station for the Dutch East India Company at the Cape in 1652. Portuguese voyager Bartholomeu Dias had rounded the Cape almost two centuries earlier. And before Dias, Chinese mariners had sailed these coasts. When Dias paused at Mossel Bay (some 100 kilometres to the west of Knysna) to stock up on fresh water, the Khoikhoi herders initially fled with their livestock when they saw the strangers.

One day, though, as Dias and his men were drawing water from the Khoikhoi's watering place, the herders attempted to defend their 'property' by throwing stones at the intruders. Dias reacted by firing a crossbow at one of the Khoikhoi, and killed the man. This incident, six hundred years ago, marked the first recorded fatal interaction between the white man and the people of the southern Cape.

A decade later, Vasco da Gama opened the trade route to the East on his successful voyage to India, during which he also paused at Mossel Bay to load fresh water. In another dispute with the herders, two small cannons were fired. The herders, terrified, dropped their weapons and fled while Da Gama's people continued to draw water.

By helping themselves at the watering place, the actions of Dias and Da Gama would have been viewed as extremely disrespectful and ill mannered by the Khoikhoi herders. What the Portuguese did not know was that the group of herders who kept the watering place open for the collection of water, saw themselves as the 'custodians' of the place. A request for water from outsiders would normally be granted, with a gift being offered to the owners of the watering place.

Although the Khoikhoi and the San resisted and attacked the early settlers at times, ultimately they had no defence against a hidden foe brought by the white people. Their intricate knowledge of medicinal plants and their immune systems could not protect them from the virulent smallpox virus brought by a visiting ship, a disease they had never encountered before.

Over thousands of years, smallpox outbreaks have occurred from time to time in the Western world and the overall fatality rate is historically estimated to be about 30 per cent. On the southern tip of Africa, however, where the virus was previously unknown, its effects were devastating. Of these effects, it has been written that: 'The smallpox epidemic in 1713 was the biggest single step in the destruction of South Africa's native San (and Khoikhoi) people by the European settlers.'[6]

Catastrophe caused by the spread of disease also occurred with the arrival of the European settlers in the Americas. Diseases spread from tribe to tribe in advance of the settlers, killing an estimated 95 per cent of the Native American population. The same occurred with the British establishment of Sydney in Australia, where a series of epidemics decimated the Aboriginal Australians.

The Khoikhoi and the San were massively affected by the smallpox epidemic which resulted in the virtual disappearance of these people from parts of the Cape. At the same time, the herders' livestock was being reduced greatly by drought and stock epidemics. Smallpox was to return in subsequent years and this gnawed away at the people's numbers, and their psyche.

Settler expansion took away the herders' lands and soon their most important herding areas and hunting grounds were lost. By 1731, Dutch commandos were actively hunting down and killing all the San men they could find, capturing the women and children to be 'tamed' as servants for the settlers. The San were regarded as vermin.

A great many of the San could not be 'tamed', however, holding freedom in their hearts and seeking to escape bondage. Swedish traveller Andreas Sparrman wrote the following about this in 1785: 'Detesting all manner of labour, and . . . having been used to a wandering life, subject to no control, he (the San) most sensibly feels the want of liberty.'

---

[6] J M Diamond (1997), *Guns, Germs and Steel: the fates of human societies*. W W Norton, New York.

In much of the Cape the San were viewed as 'unprofitable slaves'. The destruction of the San has been described as being:

> . . . of all the beastly episodes in this history, few are comparable with those involving the indigenous San, the Bushmen . . . In effect they came to be seen as vermin . . . marked out for destruction as a people.[7]

The following tells of some of the atrocities that took place:

> Commandos . . . entered Bushmanland from the Roggveld side. The Europeans went in the direction of the present village of Kenhardt and killed 200 Bushman women and children – almost all they came across. On another occasion, according to one of the witnesses . . . (The Boers) surrounded the place during the night, spying the Bushmen's fires. At daybreak firing commenced and it lasted until the sun was up a little way.
>
> The commando party loaded and fired and reloaded many times before they were finished. A great many people – women and children – were killed that day. The men were absent. Only a few little children escaped and they were distributed among the people composing the commando.[8]

In the 1790s, a travelling colonist was asked whether he had encountered trouble with the San on the road. He replied 'with as much composure and indifference as if he had been speaking of partridges "that he had only shot four".'[9] It is recorded that one colonist boasted that he personally had killed nearly three hundred San.

Colonists hunted the San in small groups, and it has been recorded that when one particular group of farmers were about to set out to hunt San people they 'prepared themselves for the enterprise by singing three or four hymns . . . and drinking each a glass of brandy'.[10]

---

[7] Dan Jacobson (1994), *The Electronic Elephant*. Hamish Hamilton, London.
[8] J S Marais (1957), *The Cape Coloured People: 1652-1937*. Witwatersrand University Press, Johannesburg.
[9] Eve Palmer (1966), *The Plains of Camdeboo*. Collins.
[10] Ibid.

By 1809 the San, the Khoikhoi and other indigenous people were answerable to their colonial masters. The San and Khoikhoi who had not been incorporated into the settlers' labour force, tried to seek space inland but there, too, they were followed and displaced by the advancing settlers. It was the end of the way of life that these people had once known.

'But,' I asked myself as I paused on the mountain slopes and in the forest's depths, 'what became of the last San who once shared this land with the elephants? Did some seek refuge here like the Knysna elephants, remaining undetected for decades?' This question nagged me as I increasingly found evidence of secret elephants that had somehow survived to the present day, while their human contemporaries had not.

One day I contacted well-known South African archaeologist Janette Deacon and asked her whether the last San might have sought refuge in the Knysna forests and mountains. Just as the elephants had. She replied:

> Yes, Gareth, it is indeed possible that San people inhabited the forest and its margins for many thousands of years and were still living in the forest and mountains after European contact in the 1700s. This contact would have had a dramatic impact on San society, but this still has to be fully researched. The only oral history about the contact period that we were able to find was a story told by farmers in the Kouga mountains inland of Joubertina at a place called Skrikrivier. The Ferreiras were one of the families. They said that their grandfathers had shot the last 'Bushmen' in a cave there, possibly as late as 1880. My husband, Hilary, went there with them in 1967 and verified that there were indeed human bones at the site. The story was that the band consisted of about eighteen people. It was said that the band had walled themselves into a rock shelter and that they were killed when the commando set fire to the bush at the entrance, trapping them inside. There was no wall at the cave entrance in 1967, but the back wall showed signs of fire damage, although this could have been the result of natural veld fires, which must have occurred in the valley from time to time. Glass trade

beads on the floor of the shelter indicated that it had been occupied after European colonisation.

After hearing Janette's response to my question, I consulted a detailed map of the area. The deaths of the eighteen people had taken place only 80 kilometres or so from where I had followed the elephant's footprints on top of the Jonkersberg Mountain.

And so it seems that some of the San people *did* survive here for a while, living elusive lives in the Knysna forests and in the mountains. Just like the elephants.

E L E V E N

The Ivory Hunters

The almost total demise of the elephant in the region (the southern Cape) was undeniably brought about by the direct actions of people of European descent.[11]

Just as the San had no resistance to persecution and epidemics, the elephants of the southern Cape had no resistance to the settlers and their guns. The elephants had previously had little to fear from humans. Before the arrival of the settlers, the San would simply have made way for elephants. Now the new intruders were waging a war upon the elephants. It was recorded in 1736 that elephant hunters would be away from their bases in Cape Town for eight or nine months before: '. . . returning with their wagons laden with ivory . . . these people were very reticent upon the subject of routes and their hunting grounds . . .'[12]

There was a great demand for ivory in Europe, and consequently elephants were almost entirely eradicated from settled lands in what is present day South Africa. The only restriction placed on elephant shooting was that each hunter had to pay two shillings and a penny

[11] A Boshoff, J Skead & G Kerley, Elephants in the broader Eastern Cape: An historical overview. In: G Kerley, S Wilson & A Massey (eds), *Elephant conservation and management in the Eastern Cape.* Proceedings of a workshop held at the University of Port Elizabeth, 5 February 2002. Terrestrial Ecology Research Unit, University of Port Elizabeth Report No 35, 3-15.
[12] G McCall Theal (1919), *History and Ethnography of Africa South of the Zambezi before 1795.*

for a licence . . .

Some of the grim killings of elephants were recorded, written about by the hunters themselves. Gordon Cumming was one such hunter/writer. During one hunt, Cumming wounded a large bull elephant. The elephant moved slowly towards a tree. There, in great pain, it remained. Cumming then busied himself lighting a fire and brewing some coffee.

The following is Cumming's own description of what took place:

> Having refreshed myself, taking observations of the elephant's spasms and writhings between sips, I resolved to make experiments on vulnerable points, and approaching very near, I fired several bullets at different parts of his enormous skull. He only acknowledged the shots by a salaam-like movement of his trunk, with the point of which he gently touched the wounds with a striking and peculiar action.
>
> Surprised and shocked to find I was only prolonging the sufferings of the noble beast, which bore his trials with such dignified composure, I resolved to finish the proceedings with all possible despatch, and accordingly opened fire on him from the left side. Aiming at the shoulder, I fired six shots with the two-grooved rifle, which must have eventually proved mortal, after which I fired six shots at the same part with the Dutch six-pounder.
>
> Large tears now trickled down from his eyes, which he slowly shut and opened; his colossal frame quivered convulsively. And falling to his side he expired.[13]

By the time Livingstone travelled in southern Africa during the 1840s, the elephants knew only too well what people and the sound of shots represented. Livingstone recorded that: '. . . they would take alarm at a distance of a mile, and begin to run if a shot is fired even at a longer distance.'[14]

---

[13] Gordon R Cumming (1857), *Five Years of a Hunter's Life in the Far Interior of South Africa*. London.
[14] David Livingstone (1857), *Missionary Travels*. Ward Lock & Co., London.

The extent of the massacre of southern Africa's elephants is staggering. But what is even harder to imagine is the suffering that took place, considering the number of shots that were fired each time to kill a single elephant.

The following is an account by David Livingstone that demonstrates the appalling suffering endured by elephants during those times. In this particular incident, Livingstone was acting to relieve the suffering of an elephant, but still it suffered unimaginable torture.

> Before we reached Mburuma, my men went to attack a troop of elephants, as they were much in need of meat. When the troop began to run, one of them fell into a hole, and before he could extricate himself an opportunity was afforded for all the men to throw their spears. When he rose he was like a huge porcupine, for each of the seventy or eighty men had discharged more than one spear at him. As they had no more, they sent for me to finish him. In order to put him at once out of pain, I went to within twenty yards, there being a bank between us which he could not readily climb.

> I rested the gun upon an anthill, so as to take a steady aim; but though I fired twelve bullets, all I had, into different parts, I could not kill him. As it was becoming dark I advised my men to let him stand, being sure of finding him dead in the morning; but though we searched all the next day, and went more than ten miles we never saw him again . . .

In his book *Travel and Adventure in South-East Africa* the famous hunter Frederick Selous, wrote about the great difficulty of actually killing elephants:

> There are, however, no animals with which I am acquainted so extraordinary tenacious of life . . . It is only necessary to read Gordon Cumming's accounts of elephant-shooting to see how difficult it sometimes is to kill these animals. If my memory serves me, he relates having fired thirty-seven bullets from a heavy 10-bore rifle into one elephant that had been crippled by a broken shoulder. I have known personally many of the old Boer hunters of the last

generation and there was not one of them who had not endless stories of elephants he had lost, after firing many shots into them with heavy smooth-bore guns.

The number of wounded elephants wandering the subcontinent can only be imagined.

Selous tells of the number of bullets required to eventually kill an elephant during one particular hunt:

> At the tenth shot he turned and faced me, throwing blood in streams from his trunk. I then fired two more shots into his chest, when he reeled backwards, shook his head making his huge ears rattle against his sides, and then fell heavily to the earth.

By the time Selous had reached the shores of southern Africa, the days of the great herds of elephants were already over. When he arrived in 1871, an eager nineteen-year-old about to set out in search of elephants and adventure, the 'old hand' ivory hunters were already looking for other occupations.

The end of the game had already been reached in southern Africa. Elephant numbers had declined to the extent that it was becoming difficult to make a living as an ivory hunter. A decade later, the situation had become even worse. Selous lamented the situation when he wrote the following in 1881:

> I had already spent ten years of my life elephant-hunting in the interior, and every year elephants were becoming scarcer and wilder south of the Zambezi, so that it had become almost impossible to make a living by hunting at all. Was the game worth the candle? . . . would it not be better . . . to bid adieu to savage beasts and barbarous men, and settle down and become a respectable citizen?

Selous did not 'settle down', though. He continued to hunt in southern Africa, making his living by collecting specimens for museums and private collectors. But the ivory trail was simply no longer profitable. There were too few elephants.

T W E L V E

Tsitsikamma, a Last Stronghold

When I was not in the forests and mountain fynbos gathering information on the present day Knysna elephants, I spent much time delving into the history of this relic population. Interestingly, I learnt that the Swedish traveller Andreas Sparrman recorded in 1775 that elephants had been almost entirely wiped out in what he referred to as 'Outeniqualand'. In those days the term 'Outeniqualand' was used to describe the very same region where, two hundred and twenty-six years later, I was discovering that, remarkably, elephants still existed. This illustrated yet again what extraordinary survivors the Knysna elephants are.

Outeniqualand consists of a 200-kilometre strip of forest, fynbos, lakes and lagoons that are parcelled between the Outeniqua and Tsitsikamma Mountain ranges and the blue infinity of the Indian Ocean. The word 'Outeniqua' derives from the early Dutch name for to the Khoikhoi people who lived in this area.

In 1775, Sparrman wrote:

> The elephants are now, by being shot at continually, in a great measure expelled from the Houtniquas (Outeniqua mountain range) and have taken refuge on the other side of the Keurebooms-rivier in the woody and almost entirely unexplored country of the Sitsikamma.

The 'Sitsikamma' referred to by Sparrman is a dense forest complex some 20 kilometres along the coast from the Knysna forest. Much of the forest today falls under the Tsitsikamma National Park and its adjoining areas. For many years the Tsitsikamma forests were one of the last, secret places for a relatively large number of elephants. These dense forests with their deep gorges proved to be a formidable barrier to the settlers and ivory hunters alike, and it was only as late as 1879, almost a century after Sparrman had travelled in these parts, that road building first began in the forests.

By the time the first road through the area was completed in 1884, however, the elephants of Tsitsikamma had gone.

A century before Sparrman recounted how two Khoikhoi men had attempted to make their way through the dense Tsitsikamma forests. After twelve exhausting days the men had to turn back; the forests had defeated them. Their stories about what they had encountered in the forest, recorded by Sparrman, gives us a clear insight that this was indeed a last refuge, not only for the elephants, but also for the buffalo that had once been so abundant throughout the region.

Sparrman noted that the Khoikhoi had:

> . . . perceived a great number of elephants with several broad beaten tracks made by these animals but which extended only from the north to south so as to terminate and lose themselves in thick woods either near the (sea) shore or at the range of mountains which separate Sitsicamma from the Houtniquas (Outeniqua mountain range). They likewise met with buffaloes in great numbers.

Just over one hundred years later, the very last buffalo of the Tsitsikamma was killed. The animal was first wounded at a place known as Buffelsbos, and then finally killed in the deep Bakleikloof.

Two years earlier, the last two elephants roaming this area were killed in the mountains just north of the Tsitsikamma forests. The elephants of the Tsitsikamma forests and mountains probably constituted the largest elephant population in the region up until the 1870s. Captain

Harison, the Crown Conservator of the Forests, and road builder Thomas Bain estimated that when they explored these forests in 1868 at least two hundred elephants inhabited the area.

Less than three decades later the very last elephant in the Tsitsikamma was shot.

Initially, I found very few records about what had caused this rapid disappearance. Some of the elephants undoubtedly would have been shot as road construction commenced through the area, but what had caused their total local extinction in such a short time? The answers to this question at first eluded me as I researched the story of the elephants.

The following is one author's comment on the otherwise 'mysterious' disappearance of the Tsitsikamma elephants: 'Whatever happened, the elephants disappeared and nobody seems to have shed a tear for them.'[15]

The reality of the situation was that the elephants of Tsitsikamma and those of the Knysna area, a mere 20 kilometres away, were in fact of one population. Elephants, after all, can cover more than 70 kilometres in a single day if they need to. There would have been movement on hidden elephant pathways between the two great swathes of forest, allowing the elephants to walk along the ridges of the mountains inland.

In recent times much emphasis has been placed on the Knysna elephants inhabiting forest, and only forest. I learnt, though, that the elephants of the area historically ranged across the coastal plains and foothills of the mountainous region north of the Tsitsikamma and Knysna forests. Also, it was no coincidence that during my very early searching for evidence of present day Knysna elephants I found myself in open fynbos country on top of a mountain with the clear signs of elephant footprints on the path in front of me. Nor was it just coincidence, when the Kruger orphans were introduced into the area,

---

[15] C J Skead (1980), *Historical mammal incidence in the Cape Province.* Volume 1. *The western and northern Cape.*

that they very quickly gravitated towards the mountain fynbos areas, staying there for almost five years, until they were removed.

The fact that the elephants historically utilised (and still utilise) the mountain fynbos areas is backed up by an article in an old forestry journal written by the well-respected forestry scientist, Dr J F V Phillips, who was based at Diepwalle forest station in the 1920s.

He wrote that he had observed that:

> . . . the elephants roamed over a wide area, and I imagine they still do where local conditions prevail . . . although these animals were frequently found both in the forest climax and higher successional stages of the forest, they were also at home in the more open areas. In the Knysna-Tsitsikamma regions these latter areas are represented by the Fynbos . . .

As mentioned earlier, Sparrman recorded back in 1775 that two Khoikhoi men who ventured into the Tsitsikamma forests had reported finding elephant pathways extending north to south in the forest, from the ocean north to the mountains outside the forest. This was a clear indication that elephants were ranging out into the mountains two hundred and twenty-eight years ago.

Also, as already mentioned, the 'last' elephants of the Tsitsikamma forest were not killed in the forest itself, but in fynbos country, on the ancient pathways leading up on to the mountains to the north.

THIRTEEN

Death in the Shadow of a Mountain

Recently, as I looked into why the elephants became locally extinct in the Tsitsikamma area within such a short number of years, I was given a valuable unpublished account[16] of the killing of the last elephant in that area. Written in Afrikaans, the account revealed that between the 1860s and 1880s elephants moving between the Outeniqua Mountains and the Tsitsikamma forest were hunted extensively for their ivory as well as for sport.

Local hunter Daniel Barnardo who, for a number of years, had made it his business to hunt elephant and buffalo in the area, shot the 'last' elephant of the Tsitsikamma.

Most of the hunting took place in the relatively open areas between the forest and the mountains inland. The account told of how for a few years Barnardo had hired his services to 'sport' hunters, guiding his clients through the forest and fynbos in search of their trophies.

These expeditions were undertaken on horseback and with porters. Such hunting trips were not to last, though, and I suspect that the elephants learnt to move across the open country only under the cover of darkness. The elephant hunting opportunities for Barnardo's

---

[16] The written account of the killing of the last elephant, entitled *Olifant Wêreld* (Elephant World), was written by Barnie Barnardo and was kindly made available to me by Julie Carlisle of the Nature's Valley Trust at Tsitsikamma.

clients became fewer and fewer, until the time came when he no longer guided visitors, but reverted to hunting alone.

The account indicated that by 1881 only two elephants, both bulls, still roamed the area between the mountains and the coastal forests of Tsitsikamma, and that Barnardo was determined that 'these two elephants would be his'. One of the bulls was a youngster, and the other a large older bull.

Barnardo had attempted to kill the larger bull several times before, but on each occasion it had managed to evade him. One day in 1881, after tracking the elephants for hours, Barnardo came across the two bulls together and he killed the young bull. The large bull, however, managed to escape.

The following, a translated adaptation of the original account, tells how Barnardo finally hunted down the large bull:

Very early one morning in 1881 the road construction foreman sighted the large bull elephant crossing the road that was in the process of being established between the Keurbooms River and up to Blouleliesvlei. The elephant had crossed the open country below the mountains at dawn, and was moving southwards in the direction of the forests and the sea. The elephant, heading towards the ocean, as the sun rose from the east, must have truly been a stirring sight. The sight did not apparently stir the emotions of the road foreman, though. No, he only saw an opportunity here to obtain free meat with which to feed convicts that were used as labour to create the roads and passes. The foreman immediately sent a message to Barnardo.

'Tell him to come quick; it should be easy to get this elephant. Tell him it's moving south-west to the Bloukrans.'

Upon being told the news Daniel Barnardo immediately checked his elephant gun. Then he carefully packed his axe in his leather hunting bag. This was in anticipation of killing the elephant that day, and cutting loose its tusks. Gun in hand he then went to the place where the elephant had crossed the road . . . there was no mistaking the large bull's footprints. The oval hind feet, stepped into the imprint of the more rounded front feet, were about twenty inches long and over twelve inches wide at the broadest point. As he stared at the footprints in the dust he saw that the message he had been given was indeed accurate. The elephant had stepped across the road less than an hour and a half earlier.

He scanned the land to the south, where fynbos gave way to forest on the lip of the krantzes that led down to the ocean. He then set out after the elephant. As he walked he pondered why this last great bull still walked the land where so many of his kind had been killed. He wondered why, after the killing of the younger bull several months earlier, the large bull had continued to walk the place like a great grey ghost. Other elephants of this area had long ago moved away into the mountains, some, it was said, reaching the Sundays River, near Addo. Others had moved inland and crossed the Keurbooms River up in the mountains. From time to time, they roamed in the Knysna forests and also those forests near the town of George. But this one bull remained. Barnardo had tried to kill it several times, but failed each time. As he thought about this, something suddenly made him shiver.

Barnardo tracked the bull for the entire day and by late afternoon was less than half a mile from the elephant. As the sun began to lower to the western horizon the elephant suddenly sensed Barnardo's presence. The air had brought the man-scent to him upon the breeze.

The bull swung around and smelt the air with its trunk held searchingly above its great head. Then, smelling the man-scent again he turned, abruptly changed direction, and began heading in a north-westerly direction, back towards the isolation of the mountains.

As darkness fell, Barnardo spent the night sleeping rough, right on the tracks of the elephant. In the twilight of predawn he was already following the signs on the ground that he hoped would lead him in that new day to the large bull. He found the elephant's tracks on the same path on which it had moved south the morning before. It was now moving consistently to the north-west, towards the mountains.

He lost the tracks from time to time, but again spent the entire day following the signs of the elephant. He found piles of droppings on several occasions, but they were cold to the touch, indicating that the elephant had passed by several hours earlier. That night the hunter once more slept rough, his back against a tree, gun across his lap.

He awoke before sunrise. He needed food now, having eaten only some sweet potato in the past two days. Despite his hunger, he was at first reluctant to seek and shoot a bushbuck, for fear it would alarm the elephant. Then, as he picked up his gun, he thought of the explosions he had heard over the past two days. The road crew had been using gunpowder to blast open a cutting for the new road. Strangely, these sounds had not seemed to alarm the elephant. It was walking steadily, but not in an undue rush. Therefore, Barnardo went first that morning to the patches of forest in nearby kloofs below the mountains. As hunger gnawed in his stomach like a living thing, he walked slowly along the forest edge. An hour or so later he sighted a female bushbuck feeding near a patch of forest. Barnardo crouched, checked the wind with his ash-bag, and seeing that it was in his favour, moved forward. He had a clear shot and soon the bushbuck was dead. Quickly he had a small fire going, and as he cooked on green sticks, the liver, heart and kidneys, he removed the fillets, backstrap, and meat from the hind legs and packed these in his bag. Then he hungrily ate the liver and the kidneys. He kept the heart for later, and was soon once again heading back to where he last had the tracks of the elephant.

Tracking was slow that day. Several times he lost all signs of the elephant. It was as if the elephant had again sensed his presence, because it had changed direction and now was moving directly north, straight to the mountains. On one occasion, but only fleetingly, Barnardo had thought of turning back. But he told himself there was no need to turn back. He was not married; no wife would be awaiting his return. He had the antelope meat, and water was plentiful in the streams in the clefts of the smaller kloofs. And so he continued onwards.

The elephant had smelt the man twice over the past two days. The bull had paused in his wanderings and pulled the scent into his trunk. Same scent; same human. The same man-scent he had smelt after the great crashing sounds when the younger bull had fallen to the ground. Twice now, upon sensing the one who followed him, the elephant had changed direction. The bull now moved straight towards the high lands, where humans seldom walked.

On the third day, though, he did not smell the man-scent at all. The sun was now lowering. As the bull climbed along a ridge, he approached a large kloof where he knew deep below sparkling clear water flowed. He raised his trunk sensing for the faintest wisp of the man-scent. There was none. The bull moved off the ridge and cautiously headed slowly down into the kloof. On a particularly steep section the elephant went down on to his great knees, and used his toenails to dig into the ground. This steadied him as he descended. At the bottom of the kloof he stepped past swathes of ferns and on reaching the stream, he lowered his trunk into the cold water.

The bull drank for some time, then he moved back past the forest tree ferns and stopped to pause for a while. He stood there, resting, half-asleep. The sun was setting on the other side of the mountains. It was quiet. There was no man-scent.

Barnardo saw the place where the bull had moved off the ridge and had gone down to the kloof. He knew that there was a very good chance that the last elephant of the Tsitsikamma would be still down in the valley. Quickly, but silently, he went ahead on the path on the ridge to see if there were any signs where the elephant might have pulled itself up further along the pathway. There was none. Barnardo now knew that the elephant was still below him.

Twilight was seeping in. There was not much time. Barnardo decided to proceed down into the kloof, stepping quietly into the hollow footholds left in the vegetation by the bull's toes. When he reached the bottom he noticed the bull's great footprints in the moist ground near the forest tree ferns. He also saw where, as the bull had drunk, droplets of water had fallen to the ground and splashed on to leaves.

The next sound Barnardo heard was a great rustling of leaves . . .

The bull had roused from his half-asleep state. Then he began pulling at the leaves of a water white alder, stripping the leaves with his trunk.

Slowly, Barnardo turned. He saw the bull's thick snaking trunk reaching upwards. The elephant was only forty yards away and yet he had not seen it when he had first approached the stream. Barnardo knew that if he walked forward, halving the distance between himself and the elephant, he would have a clear shot. He moved forward silently. The bull did not sense his approach. It stood there feeding slowly. Minutes passed. Barnardo stopped and settled himself to take aim.

Then the first shot was fired. From all around a mighty and terrible scream echoed and reverberated from the kloof and over the hills. Barnardo fired again and again, until finally it was over.

Then there was only silence, deafening silence. Not a bird called. The bull died that late afternoon in the shadow of the mountain.

That night Barnardo camped in the kloof. He built a fire and later grilled the bushbuck meat on the coals.

At dawn he awoke, washed his face at the stream, and then walked over to the dead bull. After he had killed the elephant the evening before, darkness had come quickly and he had not had much time to inspect the body of the bull. The elephant had fallen on its right side. His tusks, though thick were short, both having snapped more than a decade before.

Barnardo fetched his axe from his leather bag and soon got to work on removing the bull's stubby yellow tusks. He must have worked fast because by the early afternoon he was seen with the tusks on his shoulders, walking on the new road being made between Keurbooms and Blouleliebos.

In 1987, one hundred and six years after Barnardo killed the large bull, a party of fern pickers walked down into a kloof on the southern part of a mountain. As they were picking fern leaves one of the workers suddenly let out a cry of surprise, and the other fern pickers quickly gathered around her. The worker had stumbled across the leg bones of a very large elephant.

But whether they were the bones of the bull that Barnardo shot, we will never know . . .

F O U R T E E N

'Jungle Man', a Life of Death

*When I got in my spine shot, and saw that the elephant had sat down, I ran up
his back and killed him with a shot in the neck . . . the great carcass collapsed
in death.*
P J Pretorius
Jungle Man, 1947

In November 1876 Captain Harison, Conservator of the Forests,
had estimated that between 400 to 500 elephants existed in
'Outeniqualand', the 200-kilometre strip of land between the
mountains and the sea.

Half a century later, though, Dr J F V Phillips, the scientist at Diepwalle
forest station, recorded the following:

> Today, practically fifty years since Harison's computation of 400
> to 500 elephants, there are but 12 elephants remaining, confined
> now to a relatively small area of forest and macchia (fynbos) in the
> Deepwalls (Diepwalle), Gouna and Buffelsnek Forest Reserve, 10
> to 20 miles from Knysna village.

Six years before Phillips wrote this, it had been estimated that
approximately twenty elephants remained, but on 11 July 1920, Major
P J 'Jungle Man' Pretorius set out on an elephant hunt in the Knysna
Forest that was to impact on these animals for ever.

Pretorius had been granted permission to shoot one Knysna elephant 'in the interests of science', but during the appalling hunt at least five elephants were killed.

Who was this Pretorius, and why was he given permission to hunt Knysna elephants when it was widely known that there were so few of them?

Shortly before I started my elephant project, I had made the acquaintance of a very affable man named Beresford Jobling. 'Beres', as he is known to his friends, is a very keen conservationist and owns an exquisite piece of land in the Magaliesberg Mountains some 80 kilometres from Johannesburg.

When I told him over lunch at his farm one afternoon about my plans to embark on the Knysna elephant project, Beres mentioned that he was related to the infamous Major Pretorius, adding that 'We don't normally mention this though; the man was an absolute killer. He had such a terrible blood lust.'

After lunch, as I was preparing to leave, Beres handed me an old book.

'Pretorius's autobiography, Gareth,' he said. 'A very self-serving book. Not pleasant reading, I'm afraid, but it will give you more than an insight into his slaughter of those Knysna elephants.'

And it certainly did.

Many people – ivory hunters, sport hunters, farmers, woodcutters, townsfolk, road builders, adventure seekers, British royalty and soldiers – all killed Knysna elephants over the years. It was the ivory hunters who inflicted the largest toll. So, in truth, many people had contributed to driving these elephants towards extinction. But when they were so few in number in 1920, it was Pretorius who almost rang the final death knell for the southern-most elephants in the world.

'Lions can be dangerous enough when they mean business, but I do not hold them in such high regard . . . as elephants, of which

I have shot five hundred and fifty-seven.' So wrote Pretorius in his autobiography, *Jungle Man*.

Pretorius was a man who made death his life's work. Born in 1877, he was a transport driver at the age of sixteen, but in the same year became a soldier. At that time, Cecil John Rhodes, together with the British South African Company (BSA), was in the process of robbing Matabele King Lobengula of his land, which subsequently became known as Rhodesia. As a trooper with the BSA, Pretorius very quickly saw action. Of this he wrote in his book:

> The Mashona showed signs of hostility, and the next morning we attacked the village where the natives put up a fight. This was my baptism of fire . . . we drove the enemy into a cave, and compelled them to surrender by dynamiting their refuge.

Soon afterwards he was a full-time ivory hunter, hunting on the upper Zambezi River for more than three years.

After the years on the Zambezi, Pretorius lived for a while amongst pygmies in central Africa. After this, an incident took place that resulted in his being detained for a year in a prison in Dar es Salaam. He was arrested and charged with the killing of forty-seven people.

During his travels, a chief had rejected gifts from Pretorius and informed him that he did not want him or his entourage in his area. During this disagreement, a number of people, local tribespeople as well as members of Pretorius's camp staff, were killed. He does not make it entirely clear in his book how this had come about.

After the year in jail, Pretorius set out again to hunt for ivory. During one expedition, human death was again to occur. Pretorius wounded an elephant, and the enraged animal killed one of Pretorius's camp staff. He wrote:

> Suddenly the elephant seized the boy by the neck, threw him into the air with a terrific jerk, and then smashed him down in front of him on the hard ground. Poor Juma lay motionless, and the elephant

began smelling the corpse from head to foot . . .

Pretorius claimed to have come into contact with cannibals, who apparently explained to him their preferred method of preparing, and cooking, humans. He also spent some time with Bedouins, and later illegally poached elephants in German East Africa. During the First World War he was the Chief Scout in the East African campaign.

After the war, Pretorius was approached to destroy what was then South Africa's single largest remaining elephant population, the Addo elephants in the Eastern Cape. In historical times the elephants of Knysna and those of Addo would have been one continuous population, with movement of elephants between the two areas still occurring up until about 1880. In 1919, however, it was believed that some one hundred and forty elephants remained in the Addo region, where they came into conflict with settler farmers.

Pretorius described the situation in the following way: 'It seemed that down in the Addo bush, though it was near Port Elizabeth and other civilized parts, there was a bunch of rogue elephants . . .'

The sole reason these Addo elephants still existed was because of the difficult hunting conditions in the dense thicket country. This is how Pretorius described the Addo bush:

> Once in this jungle it was seldom possible to see more than five paces ahead, and the jumble of undergrowth consisted of thorns and spikes of every description. A terrible country. I soon realised that if ever there was a hunter's hell, it was here . . .

At first Pretorius was not at all keen on the task he had taken on. After all, well-known hunters such as F C Selous had earlier visited the area and held the view that it would be impossible to exterminate the elephants. In the end, though, it was, by his own admission, ego that compelled Pretorius to continue with the killings. He wrote:

> To be perfectly frank, I will admit . . . that if it had not been for the reputation I had gained in the north I should have followed

the example of Selous and left the Addo elephants severely alone, but as I had taken on the job I would rather have been killed than withdraw – such is the vanity of man.

The killing began. In just under a year Pretorius killed more than one hundred and twenty elephants. He lost track of the exact number. In that time he also captured several calves, selling one to a visiting circus for three hundred pounds. Describing in his book how he exterminated almost the entire elephant population, Pretorius wrote: 'It was a dramatic thought that I had fought and defeated a family of elephants that had held undisputed sway in that bush for thousands of years.'

Fortunately he did not defeat every last elephant. There was a great outcry about the killings, with the public and the press calling for an end to the extermination of the Addo elephants. It was reported that:

> The time came when the South African Press urged cessation of the slaughter at Addo. In Parliament too, pleas were made for the preservation of the condemned creatures, which by then had withdrawn to privately held land outside the scope of the hunt.[17]

Indeed, it was local landowners such as the Harvey family and others who gave the remaining elephants refuge on their land. Had they not, it is very likely that Pretorius would have hunted them down to the very last one.

Only sixteen Addo elephants remained alive in 1920 when Pretorius finally packed away his .475 Jeffries double-barrelled rifle.

Towards the end of the slaughter, Pretorius became involved in commercial film-making and engaged a 'camera operator', Joe Albrecht, to film his hunting exploits. Pretorius had been suitably impressed with Albrecht's resolve when filming in dangerous situations. He wrote:

> I remember the first time we went out together. We tracked a herd,

---

[17] *Sanctuary*. Published by the *Cape Times*, 1944.

and I told Albrecht to fix and focus his camera. He had never seen a charging elephant before and I wondered how he would face up to the business. When he was ready, I fired and down came the thundering herd straight at us. Several passed no more than a couple of paces from us, but Albrecht never budged, and just went on turning the handle. He had pluck, that man – and we had a perfect moving picture of elephants in full charge. And the very next day we picked up the herd again, and while he took pictures I killed four of the beasts.

Pretorius wrote that he thought that the 'Addo bush elephant were a race apart', and told of characteristics of the Addo elephants, such as the tusklessness of the females, which indicated to him that these elephants were a subspecies. How much he really believed such ideas is hard to know, but it was because of the suggestion that these elephants were a subspecies that he could approach the authorities for permission to hunt a Knysna elephant. He wished to compare the physical characteristics of elephants from both areas.

Reading between the lines, though, I sense that Pretorius, now enthusiastic about recording his exploits on film for commercial purposes, was seeking another exciting and saleable 'photo opportunity'.

With permission to shoot a Knysna elephant granted, Pretorius proceeded to the town of George 50 miles west of Knysna in July 1920. With him were Albrecht, his camp staff and his hunting dogs. That evening in a hotel, he heard some women whispering that they would like to accompany him on the hunt. Ever the showman, Pretorius said to the women: 'Well, anyone who wishes to come along is quite welcome.'

The following day Pretorius and his entourage travelled by road to the Millwood forest station. Accompanied by the chief forester, they trudged through rain and mud for hours until they came to a deep gorge where elephants had been seen two days earlier. By that time it was five o'clock in the afternoon.

Pretorius instructed the party to set up camp for the night while he and the forester explored the deep gorge. When the men reached the bottom of the kloof, they came across ancient elephant paths:

> ... I found ... elephant paths almost as old as the hills themselves. Not a tree nor blade of grass grew along these paths, and I saw the spoor of elephants that had passed there that morning, travelling eastward along the line of cliffs.

Then, on the elephant paths the men stumbled upon a rare sight. Pretorius wrote:

> Tracing the tracks for five hundred yards, we came upon a dead elephant calf, three feet high, which had died a few days previously. This was the first dead elephant I had ever seen that had died a natural death in natural surroundings. There were no wounds on the little beast; moreover, he was in a reserve where no one was allowed to shoot, and it was obvious the Dumbo must have devoured some substance that had created severe intestinal trouble.

The cause of the calf's death was in all likelihood not 'severe intestinal trouble'. The height of the tiny calf indicates that in fact this was a newborn baby, probably a stillborn.

Researchers have documented incidents of stillborn elephant babies. Elephant expert Joyce Poole told me once how she had witnessed a mother elephant staying beside the body of her dead calf for three days, before finally moving away. She described this incident in her book, *Coming of Age with Elephants*.

> After attempting to lift her stillborn baby for hours, Tonie (the mother elephant) then stood near its small body in silence. It was while watching Tonie's vigil over her dead newborn that I first got the very strong impression that elephants grieve. The expression on her face, her mouth, the way she carried her ears, her head, and her body; every part of her spelled grief.

Pretorius had left things late in returning to where he and the party were to camp for the night. He and the forester 'had a terrible climb that night' as they scrambled out of the gorge on their hands and knees. When they eventually reached the campsite it was late in the evening, and most of the people were already asleep.

The following day the elephant hunt took place.

Pretorius has been dead for more than sixty years, yet his account of the killing of the Knysna elephants lives on. Reprint editions of his book, *Jungle Man*, can be bought to this day. In the book, though, Pretorius wrote somewhat selectively about the sequence of events that took place when he hunted down the Knysna elephants. The fact that the party of people witnessed the hunt, and afterwards made statements about it, reveals that Pretorius was economical with the truth, to say the very least, in the way he described it.

The following morning Pretorius sighted seven Knysna elephants in the same gorge he and the forester had climbed out of the night before. Then, rather revealing of his presumably true intentions for wanting to kill a Knysna elephant, he:

> . . . began to discuss making a cinematograph film of the elephants, and proposed to Albrecht and the Chief Forester that we should descend into the opening and make for a point where the elephants had disappeared into the bush. We could find a suitable spot for the camera, and I would then remain with Albrecht while the forester, my dogs and the boys proceed to the spot where we had seen the elephants go.

The rest of the party was instructed to stand '. . . on the edge of the cliffs, so that they would have a ringside view of all that happened'. The dogs were turned loose to chase the elephants, with Pretorius anticipating that the elephants would '. . . clear as fast as they could along their old path. Elephants never make new paths, but keep to their old thoroughfares, the road of the centuries.'

Pretorius and Albrecht had set up the camera right in the middle of the elephant path, and soon the herd was rushing towards them, chased by the hunting dogs. In his book, Pretorius describes what next took place:

> Fortune favoured us. The leader of the herd was a huge bull who suddenly appeared thirty yards away. He put up his ears, raised his trunk, and charged. I hit him, at the range of twenty paces, but my bullet did not turn him; he still crashed forward. Albrecht stuck to his camera. I had to shoot again, and this time in his ear, which dropped him.

But an account by one of the onlookers, Francis Newdigate, reported in the *Cape Argus* newspaper of 24 August 1929, tells of a different turn of events: 'Then the cinema got busy and Pretorius stepped out. BANG! and a cloud of dust appeared on the elephant's back where the bullet struck it.'

For the benefit of dramatic film footage Pretorius had, deliberately and callously, shot the elephant in the spine. This fact was confirmed by another onlooker, one Miss Cuckoo Lister, who was later quoted stating that: 'Soon after, the great bull emerged, just below Pretorius, and he fired at it in the back so as to get good cinema.'

Newdigate's account of the hunt tells what occurred after the elephant had been shot in the back:

> With a sort of a stumble the old bull continued his walk. BANG! and yet another BANG! but the large bore, high velocity express elephant rifle seemed to have little effect. At last, just as he was about to enter the forest again, the eighth shot brought him down. Pretorius jumped on his body and stood there in triumph. The bull raised his head to look at his gloating enemy, rolled over on his side and died without a sound or a struggle, as became the passing of so noble a creature.

According to Pretorius, he then saw another bull elephant charging straight towards Albrecht who was still operating the camera. Of this he wrote: 'I let drive and gave him a bullet to the head which dropped him, but it was not a fatal shot, and he quickly rose. The next time I fired at his brain, and he fell dead.'

But, according to Newdigate: 'Upon Pretorius returning to his post, another bull appeared which he likewise dispatched in about six shots.'

Pretorius describes how, after killing the second bull, the following occurred:

> We watched him (the bull) then in wonder, for he had fallen on a slope and the carcass began to roll, and over and over it went down the hill. It was a weird and terrific spectacle to see such a huge animal rolling helplessly, taking trees and branches with him, until finally the immense body came to rest against a monster tree.

In his account of the hunt, Pretorius omitted to mention that other elephants also died that terrible morning. While attempting to protect her calf, a cow elephant was shot at by the forester. It was written of the mother elephant that:

> During the night she was seen to pass by in the close vicinity of the hunters' camp, and was found dead of her wounds the following day, twelve miles distant from the scene of the tragedy.[18]

Later on, her calf and another youngster were also found dead.

In his book, Pretorius stated very unconvincingly that it was the size of the Knysna elephants that 'proved' his notion that the Addo elephants were a subspecies: 'I was satisfied – for I had proved my theory regarding the Addo elephants. Was it not patent that the two types (of elephants) were entirely different . . .?'

He also claimed that the larger bull he shot was twelve and a half feet tall, and that when 'stuffed' it would be the tallest elephant ever displayed. It wasn't, though. It was actually nine feet and three inches in height.

---

[18] Winifred Tapson (1961), *Timber and Tides, the story of Knysna and Plettenberg Bay*. General Litho.

As mentioned earlier, I believe that Pretorius's main motivation for wanting to shoot a Knysna elephant was for the sake of the film he and Albrecht were making. He wrote about the film:

> The film proved a tremendous success, and was shown all over the Union (of South Africa) and in other countries as well. So true to life was it that a blotch appeared on the elephant where the bullet entered.

He ends the whole sorry saga of the Knysna elephant killings in this way:

> And so my hunting excursions in the Cape Province terminated. They had provided me with much excitement, interest, and substantial remuneration. I bade goodbye to those majestic forests and mountains of Knysna . . .

As he left, somewhere in the forest there were two very traumatised elephants. They were the sole survivors of the herd of seven that Pretorius had first sighted in the gorge.

For the next seventy-five years, the elephants would seldom venture through the Millwood portion of the Knysna forests. Pretorius's killings there had left a dark residue, a grim memory of the death of their kind, and they avoided the area.

Unique 1940 photograph of a magnificent Knysna bull elephant (F W Newdigate)

An old 'Elephant Walk' trail marker in the heart of the forest (Dominique Diane)

Fresh elephant feeding signs deep in the forest (Stewart Patterson)

Uprooted forest tree fern provides clear evidence of fresh feeding signs by elephants (Fransje van Riel)

Fresh and abundant signs of feeding on a forest trail (Stewart Patterson)

Track of a Knysna elephant (Gareth Patterson)

Fransje looking at the tracks of three Knysna elephants (Gareth Patterson)

Fresh tracks of three Knysna elephants (Fransje van Riel)

A hidden elephant path leading into and through dense mountain fynbos
(Stewart Patterson)

The tracks of the calf.
The size of the spoor
indicates that the calf
is less than a year old
(Gareth Patterson)

Dung bolus of a young Knysna calf (right), compared with that of a sub-adult Knysna elephant (Dominique Diane)

Plant material extracted during dung analysis (Dominique Diane)

Spot the Knysna elephant! (Hylton Herd, SANParks)

Knysna elephant partially hidden in the fynbos (Wilfred Oraai, SANParks)

Knysna elephant in the central forest (Hylton Herd, SANParks)

Female Knysna elephant photographed by forest guard Paulus Makriga

PART THREE

F I F T E E N

An Elephant called Strangefoot

Trees were to tell me about the Knysna elephants.

On one particular trail in the forest, I discovered that elephants were leaving behind evidence of their presence and age on the bark of certain trees. A very thin layer of earth or mud was scraped off the elephant's skin and on to the bark.

One day as I was examining one of these marks on a forest tree, I suddenly realised that this could give me valuable information about the heights of the Knysna elephants and, in turn, I would be able to determine to a degree their age groups. As I looked at the rub marks, I tried to visualise what portion of the elephant's side would have made contact with the tree.

That evening I studied photographs of elephants and concluded that the outwardly bulging portion of an elephant's sides, just in front of the hind legs, was in all likelihood the widest part of the elephant's body, and thus the area that made contact with the bark of the trees.

After making some measurements I discovered that this part of the elephant's side is almost exactly two-thirds the shoulder height of the animal. Age estimation of elephants can be determined from their shoulder heights. Therefore, if the rub-marks were representative of two-thirds of their total height, I could calculate the approximate total height, and thus estimate approximate age groups.

Obviously this was a very unscientific technique, and very approximate, but it could still give me some idea of the age groups of the Knysna elephants that utilised a particular pathway in the forest.

One afternoon, armed with a measuring tape, I measured the heights of the various rub-marks I had discovered, and found the results to be very interesting. Eight of the highest rub-marks measured were in the region of two metres, with some even higher. By adding a third to this measurement to determine shoulder height, I seemed to have uncovered the presence of an adult bull elephant.

This bull would be older and taller than the Young Bull which had been seen and photographed by Wilfred Oraai. If the rub-mark hypothesis was anything to go by, it would mean, rather incredibly, that somewhere out there was a large elephant that no one had known about before.

The heights of the other rub-marks were equally intriguing. Several measured in the region of 1.7 metres, giving a shoulder height of approximately 2.5 metres. This is a little smaller than the average height of an adult female elephant, which stands at about 2.7 metres.

Some of the lower rub-marks were in the vicinity of 1.5 metres, giving a shoulder height of about 2.2 metres, the approximate height of a nine to ten-year-old female elephant or a seven-year-old male youngster.

Although hardly scientific, the findings were most intriguing.

Around this time, the normally elusive Knysna elephants began to reveal solid evidence of their presence. Officially, it was believed that only two elephants remained, the Matriarch and the Young Bull. But this was soon to change. The guards and I were about to discover that other Knysna elephants existed.

A sighting of a Knysna elephant took place a short time after I found that the rub-marks indicated the existence of an adult bull elephant. Appropriately, it was the forest guard Wilfred Oraai who had the sighting, which took place on 26 June 2001.

At about four o'clock in the afternoon on that day, as I was making a plaster cast of a set of extremely fresh leopard tracks I had found on Kom se Pad, three forestry vehicles suddenly sped past me. From my glimpse of the drivers' faces I could tell that something of extreme urgency had happened, and I wondered if one of the guards had spotted an elephant. I was later to learn that this was indeed the case.

A week later forester Len du Plessis and I met up on Kom se Pad and I heard what had happened that day.

From the beginning of the project, Len had regularly seen me either walking or driving through the forest. We'd wave at each other, but so far we had not had the opportunity to have a chat. I knew who Len was, as I had recognised his face from a picture in a locally published book on the elephants, *The Knysna Elephants and their Forest Home*, written by Margo Mackay.

In the book I had read that Len had been involved in the care of the Kruger orphans prior to their being released from the holding enclosure. He had also been involved in the monitoring of the calves after their release. So, knowing of Len's work with these elephants, I was keen to speak to him at some time. And that morning on Kom se Pad was the perfect opportunity.

A large man, with a big beard and dressed in khaki uniform, Len typifies what one would imagine a forester should look like. I was soon to discover that he was a very friendly and kind man, who always made time over the months and years that followed to answer any questions I might have and to help with aspects of my work.

It was there on Kom se Pad that Len told me the reason for the urgency I had observed the week before. While I was making the plaster casts of the leopard spoor, Wilfred had radioed the Diepwalle forest station to say that he had found an elephant feeding near the Rondebossie hikers' hut on the edge of the Gouna forest. This news was exciting enough, but then he revealed something else.

The elephant had two equal-sized tusks.

This was obviously very significant as the Matriarch was identifiable by her prominent right tusk and snapped-off left tusk. When the Young Bull had been sighted and photographed by Wilfred the year before, he appeared to have a prominent left tusk, and a snapped-off right tusk. If Wilfred was watching an elephant with a pair of equal-sized tusks, it *had* to be an elephant no one had previously known about. Hence the rush to drive to where Wilfred was watching the elephant.

Unfortunately, Len told me, by the time they reached the vicinity of the Rondebossie hut, the elephant had moved away. Wilfred had managed to photograph it, but when the photographs were scrutinised, the elephant was visible, but not its tusks, which were obscured by the vegetation.

Even though Wilfred had seen both tusks clearly, this on its own was not enough evidence. The criterion which the forestry department applied with regard to positive identification of Knysna elephants was that clear photographic evidence was required, and that included the tusks.

This must have left Wilfred somewhat frustrated. He knew what he had seen, and it was an elephant that he had never seen before.

Len told me that although the 'new' elephant had definitely been sighted, the forestry department could not go public with the incredible news because of the lack of clear photographic evidence.

The dense vegetation makes the forestry department's photographic criterion for the identification of Knysna elephants almost impossible to meet, and made me wonder what other means could be used. Footprints perhaps . . .?

A month after Wilfred's sighting of the 'new' Knysna elephant I came across evidence of two more Knysna elephants that no one had known about before.

Early one morning in July I walked through the main central forests in the direction of a large plantation. The plantations were often noisy places during the weekdays with logging crews using chain saws, and large trucks rumbling to and fro. At the weekends, though, these areas were blessed with silence and this was when I would explore them.

I entered the plantation after about an hour and a half of brisk walking. The track I had followed was imprinted with the marks of the large truck tyres, and the air contained the faint residual smell of diesel fuel.

Suddenly a majestic male bushbuck emerged on the road just thirty metres or so in front of me. He was almost jet black in colour, with dramatically contrasting white stripes on his neck and on his flanks. Extraordinarily, the bushbuck walked delicately towards me until it was only metres away. This was a wild animal, and he had clearly seen me, yet he acted with calmness, even curiosity. Then the bushbuck stepped to the right and disappeared into the pine plantation. It was a strange encounter.

After watching the bushbuck move into the pines, I continued along the road. Suddenly, I heard some sounds ahead of me. Initially, I thought that perhaps other people were also in the plantation that morning, but as I carried on walking I also knew that there was a possibility that the source of the sounds could be elephant . . .

I then came to a point where the road split, with one track leading north, and the other south, and it was there that I saw that two young bluegum trees had been dragged along the ground. Then, among the tyre marks and workers' footprints, I noticed other imprints. Their appearance was almost like patchwork. *Elephant!* my mind screamed, but I could not comprehend the pattern of the imprints. 'If these are elephant footprints,' I thought, 'then they are unlike anything I have ever seen before.' My diary notes reflect my thoughts when I saw the strange imprints that day:

> There were these strange 'patchwork' mark imprints, but as I was in an area that has high levels of human activity during the week, at first I was not certain about what I was seeing and feeling. I questioned that perhaps the imprints might have been man-made.

This questioning was not to last long, though, for further along the track I came across a pile of very fresh elephant droppings in fynbos vegetation just off the edge of the track. And then, nearby, I saw the footprints of two young elephants . . .

My heart began to pound. I knew the elephants would be somewhere very close by. The droppings and footprints had confirmed the source of the sounds that I had heard a little earlier. It *had* been elephants.

I examined the tracks very closely. The smaller of the two footprints was made up of the 'normal' mosaics of the creases and indentations that are found on the underneath of an elephant's foot. But the other footprints were unlike any other elephant tracks I had ever seen, and I have literally seen hundreds of elephant footprints in my life. There was something quite extraordinary about them. They were very strange indeed. A name for the elephant immediately came to mind – 'Strangefoot'.

In the early 1980s, elephant researchers in Kenya discovered that a young elephant's age could be estimated from the dimensions and measurement of its footprints. This is determined from the length of the hind feet. I had hoped to use this information in gauging the ages of Knysna elephants, and that morning was the perfect opportunity.

I measured the length of Strangefoot's hind footprint. It was 37 centimetres long, giving me an approximate age of about fourteen years. The second, even smaller set of footprints was not so clear, making them more difficult to measure, but an approximate length was about 33 centimetres. This measurement indicated an age of eight years, possibly even less. I decided to name this second elephant 'The Youngster'.

The Knysna elephant that Wilfred had seen and photographed the year before, known as the Young Bull, was believed to be approximately eighteen years old. The elephant with the two equal-sized tusks that Wilfred had sighted a month earlier was estimated to be older than the Young Bull.

And now I had chanced upon evidence of two other, younger Knysna elephants. In the course of a month, there were seemingly three 'new' elephants, bringing the minimum number of Knysna elephants to five. Provided the Matriarch was still alive.

Contrary to popular belief, these findings showed, first, that other Knysna elephants existed and, secondly, that breeding had taken place during the past two decades.

It was also significant that these two young elephants were moving together, as in recent years (apart from the Kruger orphans) the forest guards had found tracks only of single elephants.

Did this mean that Strangefoot and The Youngster were siblings? If so, who was their mother? If she was alive, why did they not move together with her in a small family group? I had uncovered exciting new information that morning but, in turn, the discovery was raising even more questions.

I decided to follow the footprints and to track the elephants. After walking only 30 metres or so, I came across another pile of droppings. I continued on the tracks, and this led me back to where I had seen Strangefoot's footprints for the very first time. I saw once again the two bluegum trees that had been dragged along the muddy track. Then I noticed three young blackwood trees nearby that had been flattened to the ground. I wrote the following in my diary:

> Nearby three trees had been knocked down, but it seemed they were not fed upon. The elephants had been either just playful . . . or angry perhaps. It seemed that the elephants had been rushing around . . . a lot of activity . . . Vegetation, leaves and branches were strewn all over the place. This worried me a little because the scene

was reminiscent of when, years ago in the Tuli, I found the body of a man who had been killed by elephants. On that occasion also there had been trampled and strewn vegetation all over the place.

The signs of the elephants and all the activity that had taken place had reminded me vividly of the occasion when I had found the dead man. He was an illegal immigrant who, with another man, had crossed from Zimbabwe into Botswana under the cover of darkness. During the night, the men had walked into a herd of elephants, and pandemonium had ensued. In the chaos, one man was tusked through the back. The other man miraculously escaped. After the killing of the man, the elephants had trampled and ripped up vegetation all around the corpse.

So I must admit that my first encounter with the young Knysna elephants that morning was not without some feelings of trepidation. At that stage of the project I did not know the ways of these elephants, nor did I know anything about their temperament.

I continued cautiously to follow the elephants' tracks which led further and further into the centre of the plantation.

The weather rapidly began to change, and soon the hills and mountains around me were shrouded with menacing dark clouds. Then suddenly I heard the elephants moving to my right. This was followed by the crash of branches. At that point, raindrops began pelting down and I decided to move away. It simply would have been foolhardy to remain where I was, bearing in mind the conditions and the proximity of the elephants.

I walked quickly out of the plantation and back into the main forest and as I did, the rain poured down even harder. Soon the only sound I could hear was the roar of the rain on the leaves all around me.

My body and mind were charged with elation and excitement as I covered the six kilometres or so to where the car was parked. It had been a very dramatic morning. I was enormously thrilled and heartened by the discovery of the two 'new' young Knysna elephants.

S I X T E E N

Encounters with the Elephants

Less than two weeks later I found dramatic evidence of three Knysna elephants moving together as a group. It all happened early one morning while I was exploring a trail in an area of plantation and indigenous forest close to the Jonkersberg Mountain.

Fransje had come with me that morning, and soon after we set off on foot down a trail, we came across extremely fresh feeding signs of elephants as well as droppings. This was exciting enough, but Fransje and I couldn't have imagined what we'd come across a little later.

We whispered while examining the droppings, which were still green-yellow in colour, indicating that they were very fresh indeed.

'Do you think that the elephant could be nearby?' Fransje asked, a little nervously.

'Could well be. This is fresh,' I whispered back.

Suddenly, there was an extremely loud creaking sound, and Fransje and I both jumped, staring at each other with wide eyes before I realised what the sound was. An old bluegum tree had caught us out.

'Dammit,' I whispered. 'It's only an old gum.'

Nearby we came across a young blackwood tree that had been pushed down, and there we found another pile of elephant droppings. We also found a gum tree that had been tusked, its bark ripped away.

A little further on we came across more feeding signs; blackwood leaves and stripped branches, as well as wattle. Yet further along the trail, we found another two piles of fresh droppings. From the abundant signs, I quickly realised that we were dealing with more than one lone Knysna elephant.

It appeared that the elephants had been heading towards Kom se Pad, the main track that winds through the central forests, so we headed back to the car to search for other signs along Kom se Pad. As we walked back on the trail, I suddenly noticed that one of the elephants had stepped off the track and had moved on to an adjoining pathway, where it had pulled a young pine tree from the ground. The elephant had eaten some of the tree's roots.

For one who is used to elephants living in dry bush country, where grass and mopane make up much of the elephant's diet, it was strange to me to find evidence of these elephants eating non-indigenous tree species from far-flung continents. The pine species were originally native to coastal California, while the blackwood, wattle and gums were all species that originated from Australia.

Fransje and I returned to the car, and then drove slowly along Kom se Pad. We turned a corner and suddenly there were elephant footprints all over the road. I hadn't seen anything like this during the past months of exploring the forest.

On examining the footprints, it was clear that at least three, perhaps even four, otherwise elusive and shy Knysna elephants had boldly walked along the road together. As noted earlier, since the removal of the Kruger orphans the forest guards had only ever found footprints of single Knysna elephants. But now, for the second time in less than two weeks, I encountered very fresh signs of two or more Knysna elephants moving together.

Suddenly one of the footprints caught my eye; it was Strangefoot's. There was no mistaking that distinctive patchwork pattern.

I examined the smallest of the three footprints, and from its size I was fairly confident that it was The Youngster, the same young elephant that had been with Strangefoot twelve days before in the plantation area.

I then noticed a large metal road sign lying on the side of the road. It was battered and splattered with streaks of mud. One of the elephants had ripped the sign from the ground and, after tusking it, had flung it on to the other side of the road.

I inspected the largest footprints and found that I had not seen them before. They were large, but not those of a full-grown bull, and I suspected that they might belong to the Young Bull, the elephant Wilfred had first seen and photographed the year before.

As we continued tracking the footprints, we noticed that some excitement had taken place. It was clear that the elephants had been rushing around – the road was a mass of confusing footprints. The elephants had stepped backwards and forwards, and to the side; in fact, it seemed as though they had moved around in all directions.

There were also droppings on the road, and we could see where an elephant had urinated. I wondered what could have been going on. Then a possible answer came to mind. Could mating have been taking place? This would explain the presence of the third, larger elephant with Strangefoot and The Youngster . . .

The mating of elephants is a dramatic affair, and one that is not often witnessed. A bull uses his trunk to test a cow's urine, and if she is in oestrus she might test his urine. Mating is largely dependent on the cow as, being smaller, she can out-pace the much larger and heavier bulls. If a cow elephant finds the bull suitable, she will stop and allow him to mount her. If, however, she finds her suitor unsuitable, she will continue to avoid him.

The actual act of mating often elicits visible response from the rest of the herd. I once watched a mating pair and observed that as the mating began, the air reverberated with the deep rumblings of the other members of the herd. Elephant pregnancy is a very long affair, lasting some twenty-two months. As I looked at the tracks and the signs of excited elephant activity, I said to Fransje, 'Imagine the possible birth of a baby Knysna elephant in two years' time. Wouldn't that be incredible?'

We returned to the car and continued tracking the elephants for the next four kilometres, to the point where the tracks led off the road and into the dense forest around us. I got out of the car and climbed up an embankment, noticing where one of the elephants had been feeding, before looking up to find that the top of the elephant's back had scraped against some branches.

I measured the height of the muddy scrape, and found it to be approximately 2.2 metres from the ground. When I stretched up again and touched the branch, I realised that the elephant was likely to be taller than the scrape indicated, as its back would have pushed the branch upwards. This indicated once again that it was the Young Bull who had been with Strangefoot and The Youngster as, at approximately seventeen or eighteen years of age, he would be taller than an adult female.

It had been remarkable to find such obvious evidence of the Knysna elephants that morning. I had taken some photographs of those footprints that were clearly visible in the moist surface of the road, and I was glad I did as by mid-morning most of the evidence of the elephants, apart from the battered road sign, had been obliterated by cars and trucks.

I had the film developed, and a week or so later showed the photographs to the forest guards Wilfred and Karel. The pictures clearly showed the elephant footprints on the road, and this astounded both men. 'Good work!' Karel said with a broad smile. He then told me again that since the removal of the Kruger orphans in 1999, he and Wilfred had only encountered footprints of single, lone Knysna elephants.

I asked them about the Kruger orphans that they had followed and, from what they told me, they had grown immensely fond of them and had been saddened by their removal.

Wilfred looked up from the photographs and said, 'I still really miss those elephants very much.'

I was convinced that something unusual was going on with the Knysna elephants at the time. They were allowing us a glimpse into their otherwise mysterious and hidden world. And I wondered why this was happening.

First, Wilfred had the sighting of the elephant with the two equal-sized tusks. Then, twice in less than two weeks, I had come across extremely fresh signs of the elephants. And twice I had found evidence of two or more elephants moving together. I had even heard the elephants on one occasion.

Then, just three weeks later, the forest guards were to have another encounter with a Knysna elephant. And not only did they see this elephant, they even managed to take some remarkable video footage of it.

Accompanying Wilfred and Karel that morning was another forest guard, Bentley, and a newly employed trainee forest guard, Robert. This was to be his very first patrol into the forest.

At that time Knysna elephants were sighted only about once or twice a year. Considering the guards patrol the forest every day, and that thousands of tourists and visitors come to the forest each year, that was quite incredible. On top of this, there are teams of workers in the plantation areas.

Prior to patrolling with Wilfred and Karel that day, forest guard Bentley had patrolled the forest for over four years, and in all that time had never seen even a single Knysna elephant. Another forest guard I know, Sam, who is the veteran amongst the forest guards, has patrolled almost daily in the forest for some thirty-three years.

One day I asked Sam how many times he had encountered Knysna elephants during those long years. He thought for a while, before replying, 'Five times, Gareth.'

This demonstrates once again how enormously secretive these elephants are. And their elusiveness has served them well. In part, this is why they have survived.

That morning the guards set out through the Goudveld forests, heading in the direction of what had once been the gold mines of Millwood. Gold had been found in the area and by 1885 the once quiet forests had become a hive of human activity. The Knysna elephants suffered greatly as a result of this concentrated human activity. Prospectors had rushed to Millwood from as far away as Britain, California and Australia as it had been speculated that a massive gold reef would be struck. A town quickly mushroomed at Millwood, and by 1887 more than one thousand people were living on the gold fields. Millwood had six hotels, a post office, banking agents, shops, and even a music hall in the business centre.

It is said that elephants were sighted from time to time at the edge of the town. Mining operations lasted there for a total of nineteen years, but the much prayed for main gold reefs were never found and Millwood became a ghost town. Many of the mining companies went bankrupt, and some of the former miners turned to ivory hunting. We will never know how many Knysna elephants were killed during those times, but it must have been a considerable number. When the Millwood goldfields were formally de-proclaimed it was thought that only ten or twelve Knysna elephants remained.

The Goudveld forests were quiet when the guards set out to patrol that Sunday morning. Many years had passed since those noisy mining days and calmness had largely returned to the place. And the elephants had also returned.

Forest guard Sam told me once that the elephants had been largely absent from this part of the Knysna forests for decades, probably as a result of the Pretorius hunt in 1920. But then, in 1995, while out on patrol near the old mines one day, Sam came across the footprints and the droppings of a young adult elephant.

'I was very excited to see this, Gareth,' Sam told me. 'It was a young elephant walking the old elephant pathways that had remained here waiting for the elephants to come back again.'

One day Sam showed me the elephant pathways at Goudveld. They are quite remarkable as initially they are inconspicuous, and not easily seen. As we were walking on a track following elephant footprints, they suddenly appeared simply to stop. It was most strange. It was as if the elephant had been walking on the track, and had then simply vanished.

Sam said, 'The elephant probably followed the old elephant pathway down to the Church Millwood forests.'

At first I was confused by what he was saying. 'What pathway?' I asked the veteran forest guard.

Sam pulled back a broad swathe of fynbos vegetation on the side of the track, and only then did I understand. There was an elephant pathway. It had been concealed beneath the fynbos. But Sam had known where it was. And *there* were the elephant's footprints. The elephant was indeed moving down in the direction of the Church Millwood forests.

That Sunday morning, the guards came across very fresh footprints of an elephant, and trainee guard Robert was very excited. Further on, they found fresh, steaming droppings. Then shortly afterwards, as they followed the tracks, the men suddenly caught a glimpse of the elephant but, having caught scent of the men, it moved away through a plantation.

There was much excitement, accompanied by not a little apprehension amongst the group of guards. Bentley and Robert were astounded by what they had seen; Robert simply couldn't believe what had happened. He had seen an elephant on his very first patrol! He had never expected to see one of these notoriously elusive animals during his first day on patrol. Statistically, this should have been impossible.

The guards sighted the elephant again later that day, this time in the far distance across a wide valley. The elephant had moved through the Church Millwood forest and was feeding in fynbos on the lower slopes of the Taitskop Mountain.

Wilfred was carrying a video camera and suggested that Karel and the two other guards stay where they were, while he moved in the elephant's direction to attempt to film it. It was agreed that with Wilfred moving alone, there was less chance of disturbing the elephant. Wilfred then set off, moving through the forest below, before heading up towards the slopes of the mountain.

In this time, the elephant had moved only a relatively short distance as it fed in the mountain fynbos and Karel, via two-way radio, was able to communicate the exact position of the elephant to Wilfred.

Eventually Wilfred heard, and then saw, the elephant.

Its great head was protruding between some young trees. Wilfred checked the direction of the breeze and, discovering it was in his favour, he crept closer. When he was about thirty metres from the elephant, he began filming.

The footage is incredible. It shows what appears to be an adult bull elephant. From the moment he began filming, Wilfred was confident that it was the same elephant that he had come across in June near the Rondebossie hut. As with the previous sighting, he could clearly see the two almost equal-sized tusks. This, he knew, was neither the Matriarch nor the Young Bull that he had seen and photographed the year before. On this occasion he was determined that he would capture the tusks on film, and this he successfully did. He filmed for many minutes until he was more than happy that he had secured the evidence he needed.

He decided to stay a little longer to examine the bull more closely through his pocket binoculars. After a while, the bull ponderously began moving away to feed elsewhere. Wilfred went back down into the forest, where he called Karel on the radio to inform the guards that he had managed to film the elephant.

When he eventually emerged from the forest, shouts of greeting were exchanged. The forest guards showered Wilfred with well-deserved praise.

Once again, Wilfred had proved the existence of another 'new' Knysna elephant. The forestry department announced that a third Knysna elephant had been found.

Shortly afterwards the footage of the elephant was screened on national television, revealing not only the positive identification of the elephant, but also that the bull had been well aware of Wilfred's presence at the time. Yet it had seemed unperturbed. This was very intriguing. Only thirty metres separated the elephant from the man. The footage showed the bull lifting its head up high to enable it to get a better view of where Wilfred was standing and filming. In fact, the bull appeared so unconcerned by Wilfred's presence that it did not even pause once while it was feeding.

It was as though the elephant knew Wilfred.

At times I ponder on this possibility. What was the depth of an otherwise seemingly 'invisible' relationship between the elephants and the guards? The Knysna elephants undoubtedly perceive, through scent and sound, and even sight, the presence of the guards far more frequently than the guards sense the presence of the elephants.

Wilfred and Karel have been monitoring the movements of the elephants for more than a decade now. In that time, they have walked thousands of kilometres in the range of the Knysna elephants. They patrol the forest, plantations, and the mountain fynbos almost daily.

Elephants are highly intelligent. I think the Knysna elephants know Wilfred and Karel as individuals, differentiating them from, say, the day visitors walking in the forest.

Daily, through walking, touching trees, urination even and perhaps sweat, Wilfred and Karel constantly leave invisible chemical messages in the forest. Perhaps even of their emotions. Doubtless the elephants, in turn, receive these messages.

The acuteness of an elephant's sense of smell is well known, and it is said that elephants can detect the presence of water from a distance of more than 16 kilometres. They can also detect humans upwind from a distance of many kilometres. Joyce Poole wrote the following about the elephant's sense of smell:

> Olfaction (the sense of smell) is probably the elephant's most highly developed sense, and they rely heavily on chemical cues . . . When I try to understand what an elephant is thinking and feeling, I first watch its trunk to see where its attention is focused . . . The tip of an elephant's trunk is almost never stationary, moving in whichever direction it finds interesting. Although we can never detect all the wonderful smells that an elephant perceives, by watching the direction in which the trunk tip is pointing, we can often discern the object of the elephant's interest . . . Chemical cues are long lasting and can function over both short and long distances.

By sensing the men's scent, whether it is their footprints or where they have touched trees, could the elephants have come to know these two men? I think so . . .

The elephants, like the guards, also leave messages, such as footprints, signs of feeding and, of course, droppings. So each day a form of information is exchanged between the elephants and the men. This could even be interpreted as a 'conversation'.

I have scrutinised the video footage taken that day by Wilfred a great many times. I firmly believe that the bull was watching Wilfred. Earlier researchers stated that the Knysna elephants have keener vision than other elephants. Elephant researcher Nick Carter, who undertook a year's investigation into the status and numbers of the

Knysna elephants thirty-four years ago, wrote the following about the elephant's eyesight:

> Their eyes appear to be larger than usual, and I believe Major B Kinloch, who conducted one of the earlier surveys, would agree with this. Their eyesight is certainly keener than any other elephants I have encountered and has on several occasions proved most disconcerting. With the wind blowing strongly in my favour on the sea cliffs, I have been spotted instantly by a cow, once at sixty yards and on another occasion at about two hundred yards.

Clearly the Knysna elephants have good eyesight, and the bull was aware of Wilfred's presence, a mere 30 metres away. But he had not reacted aggressively, nor had he retreated and moved away. He had simply stayed where he was, content to carry on feeding, and all the time looking in Wilfred's direction.

In contrast, earlier in the day, after catching the guards' scent when they had first encountered the bull, the elephant had moved away. Was this perhaps a reaction to the unfamiliar smell of Robert, the first-timer in the forest? Would the elephant have reacted differently had it just been Wilfred and Karel on patrol? I think so.

In the months ahead another meeting of Wilfred and a Knysna elephant took place, an encounter that leaves no doubt in my mind that these elephants know Wilfred and Karel as individuals, and that they know that the men will cause them no harm. If this were not the case, on that particular occasion, Wilfred might otherwise have been killed . . .

SEVENTEEN

Elephants of Forest and Fynbos

The Knysna elephants . . . are the only truly wild, free-range, unfenced elephants left in South Africa.
Lyall Watson
Elephantoms, 2003

Before Wilfred discovered the Young Bull and the adult bull with the equal-sized tusks, and before I discovered the presence of the two young elephants, Strangefoot and The Youngster, some forestry scientists and researchers had concluded that the Knysna elephants were inevitably doomed to extinction.

I had read various scientific papers and articles on why they had come to this grim conclusion. It was in part because it was believed that the Knysna elephants were confined to an area of 150 square kilometres of the central forest, and that this presented nutritional, and in turn reproductive, problems for them.

Forest environs alone, like those of Knysna, are not suitable habitat for savannah elephants. In Africa, savannah elephants feed predominantly on grasses during the wet season and browse on trees more frequently during the dry season when the grasses have withered.

There was little grass within the central Knysna forests, and thus the elephants were believed to be dependent upon browse, the vegetation of the forest trees and scrub. The forest vegetation, it was pointed out in the scientific papers and articles, contains high levels of polyphenolic substances such as tannins, substances known to inhibit digestion. This is part of the trees' defence system to counter their consumption by animals.

Afromontane forests generally have low densities of large mammalian herbivores. The main herbivores of such forests are mostly the insects that have evolved a means that allows them to feed on particular plant species. Chemicals such as tannins are found in the bark of forest trees, and when eaten they reduce the digestibility of protein in food, by binding to it. Polyphenolic substances, though, are largely absent in grasses.

A forestry scientist once summed up his understanding of the situation of the Knysna elephants when he wrote the following:[19]

> It can, therefore, be concluded that the forced permanence of Knysna elephants in the forest – an unsuitable elephant habitat that historically did not carry a permanent elephant population – resulted in inadequate reproduction rates over the past eight decades.

According to forestry records, twelve Knysna elephants were still alive in 1921. Fifty years on, in 1970, the work of researcher Nick Carter showed that the number of Knysna elephants was eleven. In 1984 it was thought that only three elephants remained, and by 1994 the forestry department stated that the Matriarch was the very last Knysna elephant. The elephant numbers had remained 'static' for those fifty years, but the number decreased rapidly between 1970 and 1984. This was attributed to 'merely the dying out of old animals' and the fact that reproduction was not taking place.

Research indicated that because they were 'confined' to the forest, the elephants were eating foods with lower levels of phosphorus than in other areas where elephants exist. It was postulated that this could be a factor in the apparent lack of breeding. To quote one scientific

---

[19] Armin Seydack, Knysna's Forest Giants. *Custos*, August 1993.

paper dealing in part with this subject:[20]

> As phosphorus plays an important role in reproduction and lactation (Groenewald and Boyazoglu 1980), the low levels of phosphorus in food plants in the Knysna forests may contribute to the inability of the herd to increase.

Believing that the Knysna elephants were confined to the forest 'where nutritional problems may exist', some scientists over the years concluded that this situation had depressed the reproductive rates of the elephants. It was demonstrated that, in contrast, other former relic elephant populations had grown substantially when afforded protection. For example, after the Pretorius massacre of the Addo elephants from which only eleven elephants survived, given protection, the numbers had grown to one hundred and thirty-five by 1987.

But the real situation of the Knysna elephants was not entirely as it seemed, or as it was being portrayed.

The cracks in the theory that 'the elephants are confined to the forest' and in turn have 'dietary and reproductive problems' began to show when the Kruger orphans were introduced to the area in 1994. When released, these elephants did not remain in the forest, but quickly gravitated to the open areas of the mountain fynbos. At that time research was carried out on the diet of the Kruger orphans and it was found that their food in the open country where they lived and thrived for almost five years had significantly higher levels of nutrients than the food the forest offered. There in the mountain fynbos, the Kruger orphans were thriving on food that had:

> . . . a higher production of nutrient concentrations and that the nutritional characteristics of their diet . . . appeared to resemble more closely that of elephants in the Kruger National Park from which the translocated elephants originated. [21]

---

[20] J H Koen, A J Hall-Martin & T Erasmus (1988) *South African Journal of Wildlife Research* 18(2).

[21] A Seydack, C Vermeulen & J Huisamen (2000). *South African Journal of Wildlife Research* 30(1).

It was also found that the food eaten by the orphans in the open country had higher levels of phosphorus and calcium than forest foods. In a paper on the diet of the Kruger orphans it was stated that the orphans had sought the open country, and not the forest because they were 'in search of a diet which was more appropriate to their nutritional needs'. This raises an intriguing question: Would not any elephant, including the original Knysna elephants, also have sought 'a diet appropriate to their nutritional needs' in the more open areas?

At the time this paper was written it was believed that the Matriarch was the last living Knysna elephant. It inferred that she and other Knysna elephants of recent times had been, in contrast to the behaviour of the orphans, restricted in movement to the forest only. Of this, the paper said:[22]

> In contrast to the translocated elephants (the orphans) which were conditioned to human contact during an extended period of captivity prior to release, the Knysna elephant (the Matriarch) was very sensitive to contact with humans. This probably resulted from a history of conflict with humans whenever the Knysna elephants attempted to leave the forest complex. This can presumably explain the fact that the habitat beyond the main complex appeared to be practically unavailable to Knysna elephants in recent decades.

But soon after I started my own work on the Knysna elephants in May 2001, and for the next five years, I frequently and routinely found evidence of Knysna elephants utilising the mountain fynbos beyond the forest complex, as well as the plantations where fynbos and forest pioneer tree species re-establish themselves. In fact, I found more evidence of the elephants utilising mountain fynbos, plantations, and forest edge, than the forest itself.

There is actually no real evidence to support the theory that the Knysna elephants were ever completely confined to the forest. Elephants are highly adaptable animals. If Knysna elephants had historically come into conflict with humans, and were shot in the more open areas, such harassment could only have taken place during daylight hours.

---

22 Ibid.

To fulfil their nutritional needs the elephants could have adapted, and entered the mountain fynbos under the cover of darkness. These are lonely quiet lands in the foothills of the mountains, not areas of agriculture with high levels of human activity.

In the past, as today, elephants could easily roam these areas at night without anyone really knowing about it. Elephants spend approximately 70 per cent of their time feeding, and the Knysna elephants could have adapted to spend most of this time feeding in the more open country at night.

This sort of behaviour has been observed in other parts of Africa. In the forests of the Central African Republic forest elephants commonly utilise 'bais', or clearings, which contain mineral-rich soils. But in recent years, as a result of ivory poaching in some areas, forest elephants no longer venture to the bais during the daytime, only visiting these important feeding areas under the cover of darkness.

From the beginning of the study, I learnt that areas outside the forest are as important to the Knysna elephants as they had been to the Kruger orphans. There are massive areas of isolated mountainous country outside the forests, and it is here that the Knysna elephants have always roamed and, indeed, roam to this day.

The plantation areas are also utilised by the Knysna elephants. I discovered that where exotics like pine have been felled, the fynbos and pioneer forest tree species are quick to re-establish themselves. I refer to such areas in the plantation as *successional* areas. The elephants, I learnt, would make frequent use of this successional or secondary growth, and this finding was consistent with similar observations in other parts of Africa where elephants (and also bonobos and gorillas) seem to thrive in areas of secondary growth.

As my work progressed, and I found increasing evidence that the Knysna elephants utilised the mountain fynbos areas beyond the forest (and the successional areas in the plantations), I came to the conclusion that it was totally inaccurate to describe these elephants as being confined to the forest alone.

This would be confirmed by my investigation into the diet of the Knysna elephants.

EIGHTEEN

Food for Thought

Who planted the tree where our ancestors were born?
Douglas H Chadwick
The Fate of the Elephant, 1992

By learning what the elephants ate, I learnt about the habitats they were utilising. When I found elephant droppings, I would collect a sample and later undertake the somewhat laborious task of sorting through the dung to attempt to identify the plant material that had been eaten.

I then hit on an idea of 'pressing' the sorted plant material using CD cases. These plastic cases were ideal for presenting and preserving the plant samples. The CD cases containing the cleaned plant samples were also ideal to take into the field for identification purposes. Today I have over two hundred of the 'CD samples', as I call them, documenting the Knysna elephants' diet over the past five years.

Initially, one of the most noticeable plant items I found in the dung samples was the 'spikelets' (the part of the plant which contains the flowers) of a fynbos plant family known as restios, or Cape reeds. This discovery was to prove to be of much significance. The repeated finding of the restio spikelets in the samples was clear evidence that the Knysna elephant's choice of food was certainly not restricted to the forest plants alone.

Restios are absent from the forest understorey but occur in virtually all habitats of the fynbos system outside the forests. Because they are one of the most dominant components of the fynbos vegetation, they have been described, rather delightfully, as the 'loyal supporting cast' to the other more colourful flowering plant families of fynbos, such as the ericas and proteas.

There are some three hundred and thirty species of restio in the Cape Floral Kingdom. They are evergreen, perennial, grass-like plants with stems ranging in height from 10 centimetres to 3 metres. The larger species are very much reed-like in appearance. The types that the elephants seemed to be eating grow to a height of about two and a half metres and the tufts of spikelets are found along the upper stems.

When I found restio spikelets in the samples (as well as other restio material, such as stems) I realised that I had to learn more about these plants, and why they were evidently so important in the diet of the Knysna elephants.

I learnt that restios are closely related to grasses, which perhaps explains in part why the elephants eat them, remembering that grass is a predominant part of the savannah elephants' diet. Grasses are scarce in the southern Cape, and are replaced by the presence of the restios. But very little is known about the biology of the restio. There is, for example, very little information on how long the adult plants live. It is also not clear how their seeds are dispersed, as there seem to be no obvious dispersal agents for a great number of the restio species. I began wondering whether elephants could be an unknown link in the life cycle of the restio, which as been described as 'an enigmatic, rather intimidating group of plants with a reputation of being difficult if not impossible to identify'.[23] Somewhat like the elephants that eat them.

While researching these plants that seemed to play an important role in the Knysna elephant's diet, I learnt that restios are very rich in phosphorus, with half the plant's annual uptake of phosphorus

---

[23] Foreword by J P Rourke to *Restios of the Fynbos* by Els Dorrat Haaksma & H Peter Linder (2000), Botanical Society of South Africa.

being shunted into the seeds. This ensures that the seeds have the best possible start to become established and to thrive. This was very intriguing. As previously mentioned, the perceived lack of phosphorus in the diet of Knysna elephants was thought to be the 'cause' of the low reproduction rate. My work was suggesting that this might *not* be the case if they were eating the phosphorus-rich restios. And, of course, the presence of the young elephants, Strangefoot, The Youngster, and the Young Bull, already indicated that breeding had, in fact, taken place.

In order to learn more about the restio material I was finding in the dung samples, I had to locate an expert in this specialised botanical field, and this led me to contact restio specialist Peter Linder, co-author of the book, *Restios of the Fynbos*. Peter had been working on restios for more than twenty years, and is probably the world's foremost authority on these plants. At the time Peter was lecturing at the Institute of Systematic Botany in Zurich, Switzerland, and he was extremely surprised and interested to hear that the Knysna elephants were eating restios. Indeed, it was the very first time he had heard of any large mammal eating these plants, let alone elephants.

It had been recorded that only vlei rats, dassies (hyrax) and perhaps the klipspringer antelope eat restios, and the extent and impact of this was largely unknown. Peter was very keen to view and attempt to identify the restio material I had found in the dung samples, so I posted a number of samples of the restio spikelets to him.

According to Peter: 'With so many (restio) species and such ecological dominance, the (restio) family is obviously of great importance, and this leads to an interest in its biology, ecology and origins.'

A few weeks later, Peter contacted me and told me that all the samples were of one particular restio species, *Rhodocoma gigantea*. Interestingly, I discovered recently that this species was also known as the 'olifantsriet', the 'elephant's reed'. This name is most likely a reference to the large size of this species, but the possibility also exists that it was named for the more literal meaning, 'eaten by elephants'.

In our correspondence I mentioned to Peter that I had been wondering whether perhaps historically elephants had played an important role in the dispersal of restio seeds, that is, through their droppings. After all, elephants had, before their extermination by the settlers, ranged throughout the fynbos country in the southern Cape. Peter replied that it was entirely possible that historically elephants could have been seed dispersal agents for restios in the Cape fynbos. As noted earlier restios are an enigmatic group of plants and it is not currently known how the seeds of many of the species are dispersed from the parent plants.

What was it that could carry these seeds across inhospitable habitats, like wide rivers, or across areas of unsuitable soil and out of the bottom of valleys, which contain soils too arid for the germination of restio seed? Future research might reveal the answer to this question. And the answer might be 'elephants'.

NINETEEN

The Secret Place of the Elephants

One Sunday morning I entered the part of the plantation where I had previously discovered the presence of Strangefoot and The Youngster. As I walked down the track, and just as I was reflecting on the quietness of the morning, I heard a sizeable tree crashing to the ground. *Elephant!*

I froze, and shortly afterwards heard the sound of an elephant feeding. Branches moved, as leaves were stripped away by a strong twisting trunk. On occasion, elephants pull down entire trees to feed upon the canopy foliage, and I think that was what I heard that day.

I couldn't see anything as the elephant was below me, hidden from view by a wall of restios as well as other fynbos vegetation growing in a plantation of young pines. I spent the next two hours trying to get a glimpse of the elephant. I tried to approach it from a plantation of bluegum trees further down the track. This proved to be impossible because of the extensive leaf litter on the ground. The dry leaves cracked and popped like little firecrackers, no matter how gently and softly I moved. I returned to where I had first heard the sounds, and again attempted to move through the dense vegetation. But it was impossible. With fickle wind, and vegetation almost a metre taller than me, it would have been pure recklessness to go any further. I tried to move towards the elephant from other directions too, but without success.

Finally I returned to the spot where I had heard the tree fall to the ground. There, I climbed an embankment and peered down through my binoculars, but again saw nothing but the leaves and branches of trees. I resigned myself to the fact that it was going to be impossible to see the elephant as long as it remained feeding where it was. And so I marked the ground with several branches so I could return to the exact spot the following morning to investigate further. Then I headed back up the track to the edge of the plantation.

As I walked away, I heard the elephant feeding again. I stopped, had one last look, shook my head, and then went on my way.

Early the following morning I went back to the path where I had marked the ground with branches. As I began walking down the track, I suddenly noticed the footprints of an elephant. It had headed up the same track. It was as if it had picked up my scent and followed my footprints.

I carried on down to the place where I had left the branch 'markers'. Imagine my utter amazement when I got there and saw that it was at this exact spot that the elephant had emerged from the thick vegetation. There, close to the markers, were the footprints of the elephant where it had stepped on to the track. I could also see the 'tunnelled' pathway in the tall vegetation left behind after it had emerged.

I wondered why the elephant had chosen to emerge from the thick vegetation where on several occasions the day before I had attempted to approach it. I can only presume that at some point the elephant had caught my scent there the day before. But if this was the case why had it not moved away? Quite the opposite had occurred. The elephant had moved in the direction of where I had been standing, before seemingly following my footprints.

Perhaps, after my months of walking in the forests and in mountain fynbos, the elephants now recognised my scent too, as it seemed they recognised the scent of the guards. Had the elephant moved to that place to investigate my scent? How long after I left had it moved there and then followed my footprints? Had the elephant been curious about my presence? How would it have reacted if I had not moved away but had stayed there on the track?

Perhaps I will never know the answers to these questions, but it was a strange, almost uncanny experience. It seemed that the elephant had deliberately sought me out.

While exploring the more mountainous areas outside the forest, I discovered a faint elephant trail that led over the foothills up towards the Outeniqua Mountains. One morning late in October 2001 I decided to explore this trail further. I entered an area I had not been to before, and there I found evidence of elephants. I discovered a special place that the Knysna elephants routinely visited. I called it 'The Secret Place of the Elephants'.

Clearly nobody had walked in this area for months, perhaps even years. The track would have been impassable for vehicles as fallen trees blocked the trail at intervals. I sensed that even the forest guards did not patrol where I was walking that day, and indeed Wilfred later confirmed this.

After walking for about ten kilometres I came across several elephant pathways that led down the mountainsides. I began finding elephant droppings and signs of feeding, strewn branches, some old and others fairly recent. It was obvious that I was venturing into a favoured portion of the range of the Knysna elephants. As I walked, I wondered why the elephants were drawn to this area in the mountains.

At a point where the trail led sharply to the north, there were suddenly signs of elephants all around me. Wattle and blackwood trees had been fed upon and torn. Discarded stems of sedges lay on the side of the track. There were old and new droppings scattered along the path. From the freshness of the signs I deduced that an elephant had been there just the evening before. On one very muddy and wet section of the trail a young elephant had clearly lain down and rubbed itself in the mud. Imprints of the skin folds and wrinkles were left embedded in the wet ground. It was simply amazing.

What had I stumbled upon here? Why were there so many signs of elephant activity? My questions were answered a few paces further on.

Near the muddy elephant footprints was a small spring. Cool water tumbled from the ground, and immediately I was struck by its clarity. Both in the forest and in the mountain fynbos country, the water in the rivers and streams ranges in colour from yellow to brown. This is because of dissolved tannins in the leaf litter. The tannins and humic acids leach from the forest floor into the water table. But this spring cascaded with pure, untainted water, which was surely why the elephants regularly visited the place.

The spring was small, only a metre by a metre wide. I bent down, cupped my hand and drank the water; it was invigorating. As I put my hand back into the water again, I saw a frog sitting calmly on the edge of the spring. He had no apparent fear of me, and this surprised me a great deal. Normally frogs leap away when you encounter them. But this one just stayed there, watching me with his bulging eyes. I was probably the first human being it had ever seen. And why would he be afraid of me? After all, he had the largest land mammal on earth regularly drinking from the spring.

Then I noticed something else. Birds flitted unusually close to me. It was almost as if they were as curious about me as I was about them. Sunbirds in particular hovered just an arm's length from me. Like the frog, they had no apparent fear. Perhaps I was also the very first person they had seen.

I had stumbled upon an enchanted, almost magical place, and it was there at the secret place of the elephants that, in the months to come, I would learn so much about these fascinating animals.

T W E N T Y

Meeting the Elephants

Dramatic encounters with the Knysna elephants were to take place early in the New Year. In the first months of 2002, the Knysna elephants once again revealed their presence to both the forest guards and to me.

Towards the end of March, Wilfred and Karel were informed that fresh evidence of elephant had been found in the Farleigh pine plantations, west of Millwood. Only rarely had it been known for a Knysna elephant to venture so far westwards.

The following morning, the guards went to the area and found fresh footprints and droppings. They then set out to attempt to track the elephant. It was to be a long, arduous day. Tracking was difficult and on several occasions they lost all signs of the elephant's passage. But late in the afternoon they were rewarded for their efforts. As they were tracking, the guards suddenly heard the elephant. They immediately froze, peering in the direction from which the sound had come. Then, suddenly, they caught a glimpse of an immense ear, and a flash of its hindquarters. After this brief view, the forest, like a huge green curtain, concealed the massive animal from their eyes.

The following morning Wilfred and Karel set out early from the place where they had had the brief sighting the day before. They tracked the elephant doggedly for many hours before finding, towards the end of the day, fresh footprints that led down an ancient elephant pathway towards the Knysna River.

The morning after that, they followed the elephant's spoor to where it had crossed the Knysna River, and where it had continued on the pathway into Maraiskop forest, a stand of indigenous forest that is surrounded by pine plantations. There they came across a pile of elephant droppings that were yellowy-green in colour, indicating that they were very fresh indeed. Both men knew that the elephant they were seeking was close by.

Minutes after they entered the Maraiskop forest, Karel noticed a dark shadow to his right, a large dark shape that was fixed upon the ground like an immense slab of granite. His heart began to pound furiously. It was the elephant! To his utter surprise, it was lying on the ground, fast asleep. Karel quickly swung round to alert Wilfred and, catching Wilfred's eye, pointed to the sleeping elephant which was lying no more than twenty metres away from them.

Wilfred moved in closer, followed, albeit somewhat reluctantly, by Karel. Wilfred was determined to get clear video evidence of the existence of this elephant and, from no more than about fifteen paces, the men stared and marvelled. This was an elephant neither of them had ever seen before.

She was a young adult female, perhaps about eighteen years old. This was yet another 'new' Knysna elephant.

Shortly afterwards the elephant's eyelashes started to flutter, and she opened her eyes. Karel immediately stepped back, his heart pounding against his chest. Wilfred, though, stayed where he was and continued to film her.

The elephant swung her head and shoulders up and, sensing that she was not alone, she raised herself to her feet. Then she saw her watchers. She stood there, looking down directly at the men. Karel stared up at her with wide eyes. His mouth had become very dry.

This is too close! he screamed inwardly, moving back another pace.

The elephant continued to stand there, looking, almost with curiosity, at the men. This behaviour was very unusual. On noticing the presence of men, one would, at the very least, have expected her to react by shaking her head and ears and trumpeting before crashing away. But she did not do this. She could have charged forward, and if that had been her reaction, at least one of the men would have been killed that morning. But she did not react like that either. She simply stood there, looking at Wilfred and Karel.

Karel's face was now shiny with perspiration. The back of his shirt, damp with sweat, stuck to his skin and slowly he turned his head to Wilfred, who was still filming.

Then the elephant moved, stepping towards them. Hearing the movement Karel's eyes flashed back up to the elephant. Seeing her moving towards them, his conscious thinking shut down and an automatic response for self-preservation took over.

Karel turned and fled.

He did not stop running until he emerged from the green gloom of the Maraiskop forest. Karel's was a natural response. They were standing in dense, almost claustrophobic forest with an elephant not fifteen paces away when suddenly it had moved towards them.

Wilfred's response, though, was not normal. He remained behind, crouched beside a yellowwood tree. Peering through the viewfinder, he continued to film the elephant. The elephant had come almost impossibly close to him. In the subsequent footage, it looked as though Wilfred had been filming from directly beneath the elephant.

It was at this point that the elephant did a strange thing. Looking down at Wilfred, she curved her trunk upwards, snaking it against her head and then she vocalised, a loud throaty rumble.

It was as though she was greeting him . . .

If I had not seen this for myself on the video footage, I would never have believed that she had done this. It was astonishing.

After this, the elephant turned and stepped back to where she had been sleeping. Wilfred's video footage showed that, for a while, she simply stood there, as if deep in thought. Wilfred remained with her until finally she calmly moved away. Soon she was out of view, swallowed up by the dense forest.

Wilfred stood up, switched off the video camera, and breathed out deeply, feeling emotionally and physically drained. Never in all the long years he had been monitoring the Knysna elephants, had he had an encounter like this one. His thoughts then turned to Karel.

Karel, standing on the edge of the Maraiskop forest, was very worried about his friend. What had happened in there after he had fled?

About five minutes later Karel heard the snapping of a small branch and the rustle of leaves. With some trepidation he peered into the forest, down the pathway that had led them to the elephant. It was with great relief that he saw Wilfred's small frame emerging along the path.

Karel sat down on the fallen bough of a tree and waited for his friend to emerge from the forest. As Wilfred stepped out of the forest, Karel called softly to him. Wilfred turned to him and smiled.

After first removing his rucksack from his back, Wilfred sat down next to his friend. Then he began to talk about what had taken place after Karel fled, of how it seemed that the elephant had greeted him. Karel shook his head in pure astonishment.

Later, as they began the long walk back to their base at the Diepwalle forest station, the men were unusually quiet. They were both reflecting on the almost unbelievable encounter they had had with the elephant.

Some weeks later I, too, had an amazing encounter. For several months I had regularly trekked out to the Secret Place of the Elephants. I had got to know this remote and quiet place very well. During this time, I had collected samples of the water for laboratory analysis. I wanted to know why the elephants were so drawn to drink at the spring. The results of the analysis did not surprise me at all. The water was of exceptional quality, very low pH and of high clarity.

'This is lovely, lovely water,' commented the scientist who undertook the analysis. This was partly why the Secret Place was so important to the elephants, and why they visited it so frequently.

During my many visits to the spring, a 'game' had developed between the elephants and me. When approaching the spring I would often place a few rocks on the boughs of fallen trees. On subsequent visits, inevitably I would notice that the elephants had removed the rocks. And I, in turn, would stack them back up again. This 'game' continued for months. Through this, I was in a sense, having a physical interaction with the elephants.

Late in May I set out once again to the Secret Place, and intuitively I knew that something to do with the elephants was going to happen that day. Three hours later, as I was covering the final stretch up towards the mountains I came across a pile of very fresh droppings. Then I heard some movement in dense vegetation in the valley ahead of me.

Cautiously, I moved forward. As I headed towards the spring, I began to see evidence of elephants all around me. Strewn wattle branches lay on the path. Blackwood leaves littered the ground. Ericas had been torn from the ground. Several young Cape beech trees had been almost entirely demolished.

As I approached the spring I saw uprooted bunches of sedge and noticed how, after eating the bases, the elephants had discarded the rest of the plant. All of this was an extremely fresh sign of feeding, and it indicated that more than one elephant had been here.

On a rare patch of bare earth, I came across the fresh footprints of an elephant. They were those of Strangefoot. The peculiar tracks were etched on to the earth and there was no way of mistaking the elephant's unique footprints.

Further along the pathway, I found other footprints, smaller footprints. These were probably those of The Youngster.

Suddenly I heard the snapping of a branch some 70 metres below me in the valley. The elephants were right there. Immediately I threw some dust up in the air. The faint breeze was blowing away from the elephants and me, so I peered down into the valley. There was movement in the dense vegetation.

I tried to see them from other vantage points, but they were masked by the thick foliage. The only thing I could make out were patches of darkness moving amongst the leaves and branches.

Very quietly, I walked towards the spring, hoping that I might see the elephants there. They had clearly drunk water from the spring recently; clumps of grass and sedge were streaked with mud. As the elephants had walked past, muddied feet had brushed against the greenery.

From the spring, I peered down into the little valley. Once again, I could only see the dark patches of the elephants' hindquarters, and the movement of branches.

I decided to walk back to where I had first heard the elephants feeding. Loud trumpeting suddenly erupted from the valley. This great sound reverberated and echoed in the mountains around me, and I froze. My heart began to pound rapidly. It felt as if I had a maniacal drummer inside my chest! I swung round to look down into the valley, half expecting to see an elephant coming towards me, but all I saw was the maze of vegetation.

I once again flicked some dust into the air. The wind was still drifting in my favour so the elephants would not have caught my scent. Then I heard movement in the vegetation below me. The elephants seemed to be feeding calmly again and I realised that the sudden and alarmingly shrill trumpeting must have been caused by some interaction between the two elephants, and was not a reaction to my presence. I calmed down and moved towards the place where I had first heard the feeding sounds.

But still I could not find a better vantage point from which to view the elephants. They remained largely out of sight. Suddenly, actually seeing them was no longer an issue. The fact that I knew they existed was all that mattered.

I then sat down on the trail on the lip of the valley and listened contentedly to the sounds of feeding.

It was an extraordinary situation. Over many months I had covered hundreds of kilometres on foot through forest, plantation, and mountain fynbos, and I had learnt much about these elusive elephants. And there at the magical Secret Place of the Elephants, two of these amazing animals were just 70 metres or so below me. Sitting in that isolated place, many kilometres from other humans, I began to feel the way I had often felt when I was with my lions in the wilds of Botswana. I felt a part of the animals' wild world. Sitting there at the Secret Place, I felt a part of the elephants' world. Though isolated from my own kind, I did not feel alone. Quite the opposite. I felt whole and totally liberated. Indeed, it was at times like that when I felt I could very happily stay in the mountains and forests forever.

I know that other people who have spent long periods in the wilds have also felt this way. In 2001 explorer and conservationist Mike Fay undertook a 1 500-kilometre trek through the forests of Congo and Gabon. This remarkable 'Mega-Transect' project took some fifteen months, and ended when Mike finally stepped out of the forest when he reached the Atlantic coast.

Mike had endured extremely harsh conditions as well as bouts of malaria. After achieving what some would have thought to be impossible (and even insane), one would have thought that he would have been relieved that the arduous trek was finally over. But as he took the final steps of the journey on the shoreline, with the ocean breakers in front of him, he was filled almost with sadness. Commenting on this later, Mike remarked that, 'I just wanted to keep walking. I wished the forest and my trip would go on for ever.'

As I sat there, sunbirds began flitting close to me, quite unafraid, while the sounds of the elephants feeding continued below me. I was totally at peace.

Half an hour passed and I heard the elephants moving slowly in the direction of the spring. I realised that they would be very close to the bottom of a pathway that led down the valley. I knew that if I made my way down that pathway, there was an excellent chance that I would get a full view of the elephants. But this thought remained with me for only a fleeting moment.

I would not risk disturbing the elephants in any way. If I had gone down the pathway, it is possible that I could have captured on film two Knysna elephants that had never been seen before. Also, I would have captured an image of two Knysna elephants together. For the past twenty years, on the rare occasions when Knysna elephants had been seen and photographed, they were always solitary, lone elephants.

But I knew that I would hate to disturb them just for the sake of capturing their image on film.

As I sat there that day, I reflected on what we humans had done to the Knysna elephants in the past: the killings, the trauma, and the pain that had been inflicted. No, I was not going to risk disturbing those elephants for the sake of a mere photograph.

With these thoughts in my mind, I got to my feet and quietly walked away from two of the most elusive elephants on Earth.

Months later the day finally came when I stopped going to the Secret Place. It was not that I did not wish to go there any longer, but rather that I had finished my work there and felt that the Secret Place should remain just that – hidden and unknown. This was the elephants' place, a place where no humans, apart from myself, came. It had been an enormous privilege to spend time there, and I had learnt much about the Knysna elephants there. But to keep on visiting would have been like betraying the place and the elephants. And so one day I finally left the Secret Place, and I have never returned . . .

PART FOUR

T W E N T Y - O N E

The Mystery, and the Baby

Now . . . the dark walker came gliding in shadow . . .
Beowulf

As my project continued it became increasingly clear to me that the southern tip of Africa is a place of deep mystery, and not least because of the elusive Knysna elephants. For example, during one five-month period of the project, three of the least understood animals in the world were found washed up on beaches not far from the forests.

The first was a Longman's beaked whale. As onlookers gathered, they could not possibly have imagined that this was only the third time in the past two hundred years that a Longman's beaked whale has been seen. Virtually nothing is known about this mysterious sea creature.

Then, a few months later, another mysterious monster of the deep was found. It was a megamouth shark, an extremely rare deep-water shark with a luminous mouth. When the first ever megamouth was discovered in 1976, a completely new shark family, genus and species had to be created for it.

Later, yet another strange and wonderful deep-water animal was found on a beach close to Knysna. This time it was the extremely rare True's beaked whale. Again, virtually nothing is known about this animal. There are only two existing sets of photographs of it alive in the wild. The first photographs were taken as recently as 1993, and the second set was taken in 2001.

These were all mysterious creatures that exist in the deep oceans. I was to learn, though, that some people believed that an equally mysterious *terrestrial* being existed inland from the sea, in the range of the Knysna elephants.

I first heard about this phenomenon when a friend, Juan, told us a very curious story. Juan was the manager of a popular upmarket hotel near the Knysna lagoon, where the majority of the guests are visitors from Europe. In 2000, a party of hotel guests made an extraordinary claim after returning from a drive in the Knysna forests. They claimed to have seen three bipedal ape-like animals.

When Juan told me this I chuckled, and thought that the people must have seen baboons. Indeed this was also what Juan had thought when the guests recounted the story to him. But when he suggested this, his guests became almost angry with him. These were educated, well-travelled people and this was not a flight of fantasy. The guests proceeded to tell Juan that earlier on the drive they had indeed seen baboons. They knew what baboons were. But they insisted that what they had encountered later on were certainly not baboons.

The guests were so disturbed by what they had seen that they cut short their stay at the hotel, and left early the following morning.

A 1996 article in the prestigious journal *Science* stated that some 4 600 species of mammal are known to exist on earth, and that it is expected that this figure will rise by at least 15 per cent as new species are increasingly being discovered. Apparently, new species of monkeys are discovered in the Amazon almost every year. Just over a hundred years ago two large forest animals, the mountain gorilla and the okapi, were still not known to Western science. New deer species have recently been identified in South East Asia. A new species of monkey, the Arunachal macaque, has recently been found in north-eastern India. Another new species of monkey, the highland mangabey, has been discovered in Africa, in southern Tanzania.

But could an unknown primate species exist in the Knysna forests?

Such animals as those reported by Juan's guests have apparently been seen before in Africa's forests. It even has a name. It is the *Agogwe*.

In 1937 Captain W Hitchens, who worked for the British Government's intelligence and administrative services in East Africa, wrote the following account of his encounter with the *Agogwe*:

> Some years ago I was sent on an official lion hunt . . . and while waiting in a forest glade for a man-eater, I suddenly saw two brown furry creatures come from the dense forest on one side of the glade and disappear into the thickets on the other. They were like little men, about four-foot high, walking upright, but clad in russet hair. The native hunter with me gaped in mingled fear and amazement. They were, he said, agogwe, the little furry men whom one does not see once in a lifetime. I made desperate efforts to find them, but without avail in that well nigh impenetrable forest. What were they?

One day I was having a conversation with a forestry scientist about San rock art paintings in the area. Imagine my surprise when quite suddenly the man asked me, 'While in the forests, have you ever come across a type of furry upright walking ape?' I said I had not, and enquired why he had asked. The scientist then told me that over the past few years there had been two separate reports of forest workers seeing such a creature.

One day while in the forest with Wilfred I asked him whether he had ever seen anything peculiar, that looked like an 'ape-man', in the years that he had spent patrolling. If he had seen something, he wasn't telling, though, only conceding that in the past 'the old people used to talk about the existence of such an animal'.

On another occasion, I was with the veteran forest guard, 'Lietie' Sam. Without making any mention of 'ape-men', I asked Sam whether he knew of any strange animals that inhabited the forest. His reply was intriguing.

He said, 'Not I myself, but in the past the people knew of an animal here that was something like a gorilla.' This was very interesting, as in 1964 the highly respected scientist and researcher George Schaller wrote the following while undertaking his pioneering study of the mountain gorilla:

> In 1959 and 1960, the Kakundakari was the focus of his (Charles Cordier's) enthusiasm. The Kakundakari is to the Congo basin what the Abominable Snowman is to the Himalayas. According to the natives, the male is five and a half feet tall, the female four feet. Their bodies are covered with hair, and they walk upright. At night they sleep on beds of leaves in caves, and during the day they forage for crabs, snails and birds. Charles claims that he saw a footprint of these manlike creatures, and one was supposedly killed in 1957 at a mining camp. Is the Kakundakari a gorilla, an ape-man, or a myth? Can large, unknown creatures still exist in undiscovered Africa?

Agogwe, Kakundakari, and the being that people in the past knew about in the Knysna forests, could they be the same creature?

The existence of an 'unknown' bipedal ape in the Knysna forests cannot be completely ruled out. I write this after learning of the investigations and research of the primatologist, Debbie Martyr. Martyr works in the western forests of Sumatra, and for more than a decade now has been seeking evidence of an upright animal known locally as the orang pendek. After five years of research and searching, Martyr finally achieved her very first sighting of an orang pendek. Ten years on, still no photograph exists of the animal. What Martyr saw that day was an animal that was about four feet tall, stoutly built with short reddish-brown hair. The animal was bipedal, and when it ran (which they do apparently, very swiftly) its arms swung just like a human's.

Of this sighting Martyr said during an interview:

> The first time I saw it I was so shocked I didn't take a picture. I saw something I didn't expect to see and something so totally contrary to what I expected. Here was a generally bipedal primate.

Apparently, the orang pendek is the colour of the leaf litter that blankets the forest floor: 'It is beige, tawny, rust red, yellow tan and dark chocolate brown. If he freezes, you can't see him,' said Martyr.

In the excellent book *Beauty and the Beasts,* a book that examines the relationship between female primatologists and the apes they study, the author Carole Jahme wrote the following about Martyr's experience of first seeing the orang pendek:

> Martyr said that seeing the beast for the first time after feeling close to it for so long caused her to cry. She felt a strong pull of kinship towards the animal; it was a relative . . . The visceral shock of kinship has (since) never waned and Martyr now feels utterly committed to protecting the hominoid from extinction.

Since that first sighting, Martyr has seen orang pendeks, individuals and even small groups, on several occasions. But capturing the being on film has continued to elude her and other researchers. Today Martyr is using sophisticated photo trap cameras in an attempt to prove the orang pendek's existence to the world. Supported by Fauna and Flora International, Martyr's work continues, and has recently extended to the conservation of the Sumatran tiger.

Recently I had a conversation about the mysterious Knysna being with two men who both work for the forestry department. One was an older man who had worked his entire life for the department, while the other was much younger and was college-educated. Neither man had known beforehand what I was going to talk to them about that morning and I had never before spoken to them about the subject. Both knew about my work on the elephants and had kindly assisted me with plant identification. Neither of the men had any reason, therefore, to fabricate what they were to tell me. These circumstances thus gave credibility to what they had to say.

I began the conversation by mentioning what hotel guests claimed they had seen in the forest in 2000. The younger man turned to me and immediately began telling how his father, who had also worked for the forestry department, had himself seen such a being. One night while his father was driving through the forests, a bipedal creature suddenly ran across the road. He saw it in full view in the car's headlights.

The older man nodded and then told me that his brother-in-law had also seen such a creature about eighteen months earlier. This sighting had also taken place at night from a vehicle. And apparently eight months before workers in the Buffelsnek plantation also claimed to have seen the same creature.

The younger man said thoughtfully, 'It seems that this creature is like us, that is to say, human-like, and walks upright.'

Recently I had the pleasure of speaking to the world-renowned palaeontologist, Dr Robert Brain. Over the years Dr Brain has investigated reports of an agogwe type of being in Southern Africa. During one of our conversations I mentioned the reported sightings in the vicinity of the Knysna forests. Dr Brain believes that the phenomenon comes down to a question of the human psyche. When people describe what they see, their descriptions are curiously similar to scientific descriptions of early hominids. Is the agogwe, or 'otan' as I have heard it referred to here in the forests, an actual proto-human from the ancient past? Or is it some kind of visual memory from that past, an image that manifests in the ancient world of the forest?

'Nothing can be discounted,' Dr Brain cautioned me.

Whatever the people are seeing, there is certainly a greater mystery here than the elephants . . .

Early one morning in October 2002, three Knysna elephants were walking along Kom se Pad. Two were young adults, but the third elephant was tiny, a little calf.

A baby had been born to the forest!

Suddenly the elephants froze. Some way up the road they could hear a car approaching. Normally when this happens they quietly step into the green gloom of the forest on either side of the road and simply vanish. But this was difficult terrain for the baby. One side of the road was flanked by a steep embankment, while the ground on the other side sloped abruptly, and almost vertically, down to a stream.

The car was close now, and the elephants began running down the track. The baby's little legs moved rapidly to maintain the pace of the adults.

Beyond the corner, the ground was more level, and after turning the bend in the road, the elephants entered the forest. They had been very fearful and as they ran the calf defecated involuntarily.

Just as the flank of the mother elephant dissolved into the mosaic of forest green, the car turned the same corner.

Then it came to an abrupt halt. *'Elephant!'* someone exclaimed.

The elephant footprints and the mushy pile of droppings had been noticed. Doors opened and a family alighted from the car to inspect the evidence of the elephants. Nearby, not more than 30 metres away, the elephants stood motionless, like great grey statues. And the forest hid them completely.

One of the people, a woman, walked along the road, following the elephants' passage. As she passed the mushy droppings, she saw where the elephants had left the road and entered the forest. Then she noticed something strange. On the edge of the road, she saw a small frog. It was dying, two thirds of its little body had been completely flattened. The frog lay in a large circular depression in the earth. It had been flattened by one of the elephant's feet.

The woman turned to look around her. A pungent smell hung in the air. She smelt the elephants' anxiety as they had fled. She also sensed the tension in the forest. A feeling of apprehension, almost like a rivulet of icy water, ran down her spine. She shivered, and then quickly turned round and walked briskly back to the car.

And all the time the elephants were listening.

They heard the doors of the car close and the gunning of the engine; the people were going on their way. They would never know how close they had been to the two adults and the baby.

The elephants waited. Then when the sound of the car became distant, the mother elephant rumbled the infrasonic 'let's go' signal. She touched the calf on its head with her trunk, before holding its little tail, and literally began steering the baby forward towards the Gouna river.

I too was in the Gouna forest that morning, and word of the elephants was to reach me surprising quickly. As I turned a corner, I saw a white truck approaching.

It was the forester Len du Plessis. 'Morning, Gareth,' he said to me. 'Elephant tracks were seen an hour ago on Kom se Pad. Thought you would like to know.'

I thanked Len and drove towards Kom se Pad. After driving four kilometres into the indigenous forest below the Jonkersberg Mountain, I suddenly saw the tracks. They were partly obscured because several vehicles had already passed along the road. I got out of the car to scrutinise the signs of the elephants.

On the edge of the road were Strangefoot's distinctive tracks. Then I saw other footprints. They were a similar size to Strangefoot's, indicating that it was not The Youngster who had accompanied her that morning. This was another elephant. As I walked along the road I suddenly saw that the elephants had begun to run; there had been urgency in their strides.

But then I noticed something else. And at first I could not believe my eyes. There, imprinted on the ground, were miniature elephant footprints, no more than about 20 centimetres in length.

Staring up at me were the tiny footprints of a young calf. From the size of the tracks, I estimated that it was probably no more than five or six months old. I quickly walked back to the car, got my camera, and photographed the little imprints. I had solid evidence that a Knysna calf existed.

At times afterwards I could not believe the calf existed at all, despite the photographs. It was just so momentous a happening. And I told no one about it.

Many months passed before I discovered that someone else knew about the baby.

Wilfred had been a little cautious of me at the beginning of the project. Shy almost, and perhaps a little sceptical. This was entirely understandable. Over the years, other people had come to the forest, some for a few weeks, some for several months, and they all set out to find the last Knysna elephants. Wilfred had seen them come, and he had seen them go. And none of them found the elephants.

Wilfred had seen them all, and all of the seekers had repeatedly quizzed him about the elephants. They had sought to suck information about the elephants out of him. I think the most frequent question Wilfred has ever heard is, 'How many elephants are there?'

He would shrug his slight shoulders and quite truthfully reply, 'We do not know.'

If I had been impatient during the early stages of the project, I could easily have phoned Wilfred often, daily in fact. I could have asked him about the elephants and what he had encountered in the forest. But I did not do this.

What Wilfred knew about the elephants, he himself had discovered, and that belonged to him. Day after day, week after week, year after year, this modest man earned and owned that knowledge. It was not something just to be given away.

Another reason I did not pester him about the elephants was because in the early stages my study was unofficial, and I did not want to risk anything impacting negatively on him. Initially, I had no formal permission or authorisation. He had his job and, in years to come, his pension. People + Politics = Problems. That I had learnt many years ago in the wildlife game.

So I quietly got on with things and did not attempt the short cut of trying to draw secrets about the elephants out of Wilfred. Instead, I walked and walked, learning for myself.

In time, Wilfred increasingly understood that I was serious about my task, particularly after he found my footprints in very lonely places in the forest and mountains.

For a short time, I think Wilfred saw me as a threat. A threat to his elephant domain, a threat to the world that he held so dear. In the Knysna area, he was 'Mr Elephant'. Not that ego was the issue, though. No, the emotions and feelings ran infinitely deeper than mere ego. It was the elephants themselves. He knew these animals and their ways as nobody else did. And for that short time I think he thought I was somehow going to take from him his intimacy with the elephants.

As time passed, Wilfred recognised that I was not a threat to him. He began to volunteer information, information that often confirmed some of my theories about the elephants. I told him of my own findings, and filled in a few gaps in his own understanding of the elephants. Mutual respect was forged between us.

Then the day came when Wilfred asked me that much-asked question, 'How many elephants do you think there are?' And I replied truthfully, and with a chuckle, 'We do not know.'

We were chatting at the little wooden ticket office that Wilfred manned during holiday season at the start of one of the public hiking trails.

'But,' I continued in a more serious tone, 'I think there could be, at the very least, six elephants from the signs I have seen over the past few years. What do you think, Wilfred?'

'I agree with you, Gareth,' Wilfred replied. 'There could be at least six, maybe even more.'

By this time, Wilfred knew quite a lot about me. He knew that I had lived in the wilds with lions. And he also knew that when I had lived with the lions it was in an area with high numbers of elephants, and that for many years I had seen elephants on an almost daily basis. Knowing this, he would ask me specific questions about elephants from time to time. He asked me about herd structures, for example, and calving rates, the longevity of elephants. At times I would lend him books and videos about elephants.

He suddenly turned to me and said, 'Gareth, the very young elephants, the babies, what do their droppings look like?' At that time, 'officially' at least, the last known Knysna calf had been born some time in 1989. Wilfred therefore had no first-hand experience of calves and their ways. Births were so few he had not had the opportunity to learn about things like what milk babies' droppings look like.

I replied, 'When the baby elephant is still really young and is totally dependent on its mother's milk, the dung is loose. It changes increasingly into little dung balls as the calf begins to eat more and more vegetation.'

Wilfred nodded his head. He looked thoughtful again, and was quiet for a little while before he said, 'I have not told anyone this before but I saw dung like that several months ago, along the Gouna river. I was following tracks of an elephant, and saw this strange loose dung on the ground. This was something entirely new to me, but when I thought about things, I was fairly sure what it was. I think there is a calf in the forest. But I kept quiet about it.'

His reaction to the evidence of a calf had been the same as mine. Neither of us had spoken about it.

So I told Wilfred that I had also been keeping quiet about something, and recounted how I had come across (and photographed) the footprints of the calf on Kom se Pad. Wilfred looked at me and smiled. With much pride, he said, 'Then it is certain. There are no more doubts. We have a new elephant! Children are the future. And this is our elephants' future!'

TWENTY-TWO

Elephants, Mushrooms, and Self-Medication

My ongoing study of the diet of the Knysna elephants led me to a totally unexpected discovery. I found that the elephants routinely sought out and ate a medicinal food item that had never before been recorded in the diet of the African elephant. Remarkably, it seemed that a form of self-medication was occurring among the Knysna elephants.

I discovered that the Knysna elephants consistently eat a medicinal mushroom that, according to recent scientific studies, contains compounds that have anti-tumour, antiviral, antibacterial and anti-parasitic properties. Current research also indicates that the compounds contained in the mushroom show exciting promise in the field of treatment for people suffering from various forms of cancer and AIDS.

As I analysed the diet samples, I frequently came across small pieces of a dark and spongy substance, quite unlike the other pieces of woody material or leaves that I found in the dung. On closer inspection, and using a magnifying glass, I determined that they were pieces of some kind of mushroom. This was very interesting. I had never before heard of elephants eating mushrooms.

Mushrooms belong to the group of organisms known as fungi, and are regarded as being separate from both animals and plants, and are thus designated their separate kingdom. Fungi are the recyclers of the forest. They consume the dead and the dying, and in this way return to the soil the minerals that literally replenish the earth. The following aptly describes the role of the fungi in the forest:

> Together with the bacteria, fungi form a vital link in the processes of growth and decay, maintaining the endless recycling of nutrients without which the forest and its creatures cannot exist . . . The luxuriant growth of the rainforests can only be sustained by the fast recycling of nutrients, aided by the fungi and microscopic bacteria.[24]

There are more than 1 500 species of mushrooms in Southern Africa and I often pondered how I was going to be able to identify the type I was repeatedly finding in the dung samples. It was to turn out that the elephants themselves were to show me what species of mushroom they were eating so frequently.

One morning while in the central forests, I came across the fresh tracks of an elephant. I followed them along the forest road as it led to a faint elephant pathway. I walked down the pathway, and then noticed a chunk of corky, brown bracket fungus on the ground. When I picked it up, I immediately saw that it was very similar in texture to that which I was consistently finding in the dung samples. As I examined the fungus more closely, I was amazed to see where the elephant's brick-like molars had bitten through it. I could see the indentations of the tooth quite clearly.

I looked around me on the pathway for further signs of the elephant. Just three paces away, I saw a large intact bracket fungus, the same kind that I was holding, lying near the base of a tree. These bracket fungi grow on the bark of certain trees, and it was obvious that the elephant, while feeding, had pulled the bracket from the tree before, for some reason, dropping it.

Through research of my own, and after consulting experts on the subject, I was to learn that these bracket fungi were of the species *Ganoderma applanatum*. After identifying the type of bracket, I had

---

[24] Isak van der Merwe, *The Knysna and Tsitsikamma Forests*. Department of Water Affairs and Forestry, 1998.

to try to determine *why* the elephants were eating this somewhat unlikely food source. Since I had never before known elephants to eat mushrooms, I decided to contact some elephant specialists about this.

The first person I contacted was Joyce Poole. Joyce was very surprised by my discovery. She, too, had never known elephants to eat fungi. She then directed me to other elephant specialists. I contacted Andrea Turkalo, a zoologist who for more than fourteen years has been studying forest elephants in the remote and wild rainforests of the Dzanga-Sangha Reserve in the Central African Republic.

Until relatively recently, very little was known about the forest elephants, and this was partly because of their inaccessible habitat. Andrea had set up her camp near a 'bai', a forest clearing where the elephants gather to feed on the mineral-rich soil. Over the years by observing the forest elephants at the bai, Andrea, amazingly, can recognise some 2 300 individual forest elephants.

Andrea, like Joyce, was very much surprised to hear about the Knysna elephants routinely eating the bracket fungi. She had never recorded the forest elephants eating *Ganoderma*. She had analysed more than 2 500 dung samples and had never come across any sign of fungus. This I found most intriguing. Was the eating of the bracket fungi a uniquely Knysna phenomenon and, if so, why?

I then contacted an Asian elephant specialist, Vivek Menon, in India. Asian elephants have worked with and lived with humans for more than five thousand years. I felt that because the relationship between people and elephants in that part of the world was so ancient, it was likely that I might find some answers there. But Vivek was as surprised by my findings as Joyce and Andrea had been and, like them, reported that the Asian elephant had not been known to eat the bracket fungus. What was going on?

It was at this point that I discovered that *Ganoderma* has been revered as an important medicinal mushroom in China and many other parts of the world for thousands of years. I learnt for example that:

Ganoderma applanatum. American reishi. Like Japanese reishi (*Ganoderma lucidum*), this bracket fungus is considered a powerful immune stimulant and strengthening tonic. There are several known ingredients including ganoderic acids (triterpenes which have a molecular structure similar to steroid hormones), polysaccharides, and ergosterols. American reishi (*Ganoderma applanatum*) and related species of this genus are valued by AIDS sufferers for the many reported benefits . . .[25]

Such information posed the questions: Are the Knysna elephants using *Ganoderma* for medicinal reasons? Was this a form of self-medication?

This led me on to research the exciting new science of *Zoopharmacognosy*, a science that is barely a decade old, which explores the behavioural strategies used by animals to maintain health. Recent studies are increasingly indicating that animals do not merely depend on their immune systems to maintain health but actively seek out certain substances for purposes that can only be described as medicinal. The seeking out of charcoal by animals is a prime example.

Charcoal has very little nutritional value but it has been recorded that a great many animals, including deer, ponies, camels, dogs, chimps, and colobus monkeys, are all drawn to eat it. Charcoal is well known for its medicinal, toxin binding properties. We humans use it for similar purposes. All over the world in hospital emergency rooms, charcoal is used to deal with poisoning and drug overdoses.

A fascinating observation of an elephant self-medicating was observed a few years ago by a wildlife researcher in Kenya. A pregnant elephant was monitored for almost a year. In that time she ate a normal diet and roamed about the same distance each day of approximately five kilometres. Then, towards the end of the gestation period, the elephant suddenly trekked almost 30 kilometres in a single day to a tree belonging to the Boraginaceae family. The elephant proceeded to eat the entire tree! Four days later she gave birth to a healthy calf.

---

[25]   Suzanne Diamond (2000), *Beauty in Peril – the Stoltmann Wilderness*. *HerbalGram* 48: 50-62.

The researcher subsequently discovered that traditionally Kenyan women would brew a tea from the leaves of this tree. The purpose? To induce labour.

One of the most famous examples of animals self-medicating has been observed in chimpanzees. World-famous primatologist Jane Goodall studied the Gombe chimps in Tanzania for almost forty years. And it was at Gombe that researchers observed chimps self-medicating.

The chimps were thought to be susceptible to intestinal worms, but the researchers at Gombe learnt how they dealt with this potential health hazard. The chimps would very carefully select leaves of a particular tree, *Aspilia rudis*, the leaves of which are rough in texture and are not part of the chimps' normal diet.

When the leaf has been chosen, the chimp will carefully fold it and keep it in its mouth for several seconds, before swallowing it whole. Clearly this was not normal feeding behaviour. It was thought that the leaves might contain compounds that would destroy the intestinal worms, particularly as it was learnt from the local people that they too used the leaves of this tree for medicinal purposes. Analysis did indeed show that the leaves contained a chemical known for its antibacterial and antifungal properties. But was there a sufficient amount of this chemical in the swallowed leaves to be effective in ridding chimps of intestinal worms?

Some years later Professor Michael Huffman discovered how the chimps were self-medicating with the coarse leaves. On inspecting excreted swallowed leaves, he noticed that the intestinal worms had literally 'hooked' on to the tiny barbs that cover the surfaces of the leaves. The worms were thus caught on the barbs and were then expelled from the chimp's body.

Since this discovery, medicinal leaf swallowing has been observed in more than eleven chimp, bonobo, and eastern lowland gorilla populations throughout equatorial Africa.

Clay is another medicine used by animals (as well as human beings).

A detoxifying substance that not only binds toxins, clay can also act as an antacid, protecting the stomach lining. Wild animals worldwide consume clay for medicinal reasons. In Africa, for example, monkeys, chimps, elephants and many other animals eat clay to deal with toxins contained in their diet. In South America, macaws, monkeys, deer, tapirs and others also eat clay.

Recent research has revealed that the consumption of soil by elephants might minimise the toxic effects of compounds found in forest browse. As I have mentioned before, many of the forest plants contain chemical compounds that reduce the digestibility of protein in food by binding it. Elephants living in the cloud forest of Ngorongoro Conservation Area in Tanzania might minimise the effects of these compounds by eating soil found at a series of cliffs that they regularly visit at night. Research has revealed that this soil contains 36 per cent kaolin, a mineral that has been used for medicinal purposes for centuries and which absorbs toxic substances in the stomach. In Britain, kaolin is used in the treatment of stomach disorders associated with alkaloid and food poisoning.

So it appears that the Ngorongoro elephants are self-medicating with this soil to neutralise the activity of many plant compounds. As clay remains bound to the mucous layer of the gut for some time after being ingested, it can continue to benefit the elephant by adsorbing toxins and protecting the gut lining.

People, too, use clay for medicinal reasons and to remove toxic alkaloids in foods. In Australia, for example, Aborigines cook clay with certain roots to remove their otherwise bitter taste. Native American people do the same thing when cooking wild potatoes. By cooking with clay, the toxic alkaloids in the wild potatoes are removed.

Returning to primates, I learnt that gorillas and chimps are also known to eat, and in fact to relish, *Ganoderma applanatum*. But, as with the Knysna elephants, it was not known why.

Dian Fossey wrote the following about gorillas eating *Ganoderma* in her famous book, *Gorillas in the Mist*.

Still another special food (of the gorillas) is bracket fungus (*Ganoderma applanatum*), a parasitical tree growth resembling a large solidified mushroom. The shelf like projection is difficult to break free from a tree, so younger animals often have to wrap their arms and legs awkwardly around a trunk and content themselves by only gnawing at the delicacy. Older animals that succeed in breaking the fungus loose have been observed carrying it several hundred feet from its source, all the while guarding it possessively from more dominant individuals' attempts to take it away. Both the scarcity of the fungus and the gorillas liking of it cause intergroup squabbles, a number of which are settled by the Silverback, who simply takes the item of contention for himself.

Dian Fossey also described what occurred while she was walking in the forest with two young orphaned gorillas that suddenly spied several brackets on a tree. The youngsters immediately became very excited and quickly climbed into the tree, attempting to consume the hard fungus.

Fossey wrote about what took place after the orphans had eaten some of the *Ganoderma*: 'Reluctantly they descended, but as we walked on, they gazed longingly back at the tree with the fungus elixir.'

According to Richard W Byrne, professor of evolutionary psychology at the University of St Andrews, the eating of fungus is something of a puzzle in primate research circles. He commented on this after reading some of my early findings on the fact that Knysna elephants were eating *Ganoderma*.

Professor Byrne felt that although in theory medicinal use of *Ganoderma* could well explain the reason why the great apes eat the fungus, research had not yet been undertaken in this field and therefore there was no hard data to support the theory.

Byrne, like Dian Fossey, also commented that gorillas would excitedly grab and monopolise any *Ganoderma* they chanced upon. Something about *Ganoderma* clearly excites these apes, and it is doubtful that it is because of its taste. *Ganoderma* is not pleasant to taste, at least not to human beings, because it is tough, corky in texture and somewhat bitter. Despite this, gorillas eat it with apparent relish.

Byrne commented that perhaps it was eaten to absorb poisons, in the way that Fuller's Earth is used in human treatments. But, he added, if it was a case of dealing with toxin accumulations, one would expect gorilla families, being social animals, to visit places where the entire family group can benefit from the substance, much like the elephants at the cliffs in the Ngorongoro Conservation Area.

I discovered that this kind of behaviour does indeed occur in gorillas. Back in 1963, George Schaller observed that gorillas 'mine' yellow volcanic rock in the Virunga Mountains. They pull off small chunks of the rock and grind it in their hands before eating it. Recent research has revealed that this rock contains clay that is similar to kaolin, and therefore possibly similarly absorbs toxins and protects the gut lining.

For now, at least, there is no scientific explanation as to why gorillas and other African great apes eat *Ganoderma*. When the answer is found one day, I would not be surprised if it was learnt that they self-medicate with this mushroom.

Returning to the Knysna elephants. As I researched the medicinal mushrooms it became increasingly probable that the elephants were routinely eating the bracket fungi for reasons relating to health maintenance.

I learnt, for example, that certain mushrooms are a rich source of natural antibiotics. Hence it is increasingly substantiated that corky polypore mushrooms such as *Ganoderma* provide an immunological shield against a variety of infectious diseases. Medicinal mushrooms like *Ganoderma* are also an excellent source of B-complex vitamins, such as thiamine, riboflavin, niacin and pantothenic acid. In addition, they are said to be loaded with minerals such as phosphorus, iron, selenium, calcium, potassium and sodium.

Ganoderma applanatum is one of six types of *Ganoderma* that has been used in traditional Chinese medicine for thousands of years. It has been estimated that some 270 species of mushroom are known for their medicinal value, while another 1 800 species have been identified with potential medicinal properties. It seems that *Ganoderma* has the longest historical record of medicinal usage, dating back at least four thousand years. In China and Korea, *Ganoderma* is known as Ling Zhi, 'The Mushroom of Longevity'.

Recent figures show that some 4 300 tonnes of *Ganoderma lucidum*, or reishi, are cultivated annually in the East, with an estimated 4.3 million people worldwide using it today for its apparent health properties. Such figures will only increase as the Western world acknowledges the health benefits of medicinal mushrooms. It has been reported, for example, that in 1991 the annual world market value of medicinal mushrooms was approximately US$ 1.2 million. By 1994 this had risen to 3.6 million, and then to 6.0 million in 1999.

Though extremely well known and revered for medicinal properties in the East, it is only in very recent years that the medical world in the West has begun to pay attention to its properties. Traditional medical researchers in the West had, until very recently, ignored medicinal mushrooms. But with increased research taking place, medicinal mushrooms could soon become a major factor in complementary medicine in the West.

So seriously is the Western medical world now investigating the medicinal value of mushrooms, that in August 2002 the organisation Cancer Research UK produced what is regarded as the world's most comprehensive review on how medicinal mushrooms are used in Japan, China, and Korea. The 256-page report[26] tells of how mushrooms could herald a new era of cancer treatment and prevention, and that the Western world can learn from the ancient medicinal knowledge of mushrooms in the East. In the report it was noted that:

> Over the last 2-3 decades scientific and medical studies have been
> carried out in Japan, China, Korea and more recently in the USA

---

[26] Smith, Rowan & Sullivan, *Medicinal Mushrooms: Their therapeutic properties and current medical usage with special emphasis on cancer treatments.* Cancer Research UK, May 2002.

which have increasingly demonstrated the potent and unique health enhancing properties of compounds extracted from a range of medicinal mushrooms. Explanations of how such compounds function in animal and human systems are now regularly appearing in peer-reviewed scientific and medicinal journals . . . Human epidemiological studies in Japan and Brazil strongly suggest that regular consumption of certain medicinal mushrooms over prolonged periods of time significantly reduces the levels of cancer incidence . . .

In the final summary of the report it was stated that:

This Report has demonstrated that many mushroom species (the medicinal mushrooms) contain some unique and intriguing biochemical compounds that have undergone controlled clinical studies in Asian and some Western research institutions and hospitals, demonstrating considerable effectiveness in the treatment of many diseases, especially cancer.

One of the authors of the Cancer Research UK report, Professor John Smith, stated that:

There is now increasing evidence that the medicinal mushrooms offer a remarkable array of medicinally important compounds that have yet to be evaluated by Western medical scientists.

Co-author of the report Dr Richard Sullivan said:

A vast amount of information has been collated which suggests that compounds derived from mushrooms could have a hugely beneficial influence on the way cancer is treated.

Of the findings of the report Sir Paul Nurse, Chief Executive of Cancer Research UK, said:

The information coming out of the East about the apparent benefits of mushrooms for health and the potential to help treat cancer patients is very interesting. More work needs to be done on how mushrooms can be used in Western medicine. This report gives weight to the argument for clinical trials to be set up to try to validate research done in other parts of the world.

Just months before the release of the extensive Cancer Research UK's report on the therapeutic properties of medicinal mushrooms, other senior figures in medical research also commented on the health-giving properties of mushrooms, and their medicinal use in the East. Dr John Wilkinson,[27] for example, of the Herbal Medicine Department at Middlesex University was quoted in a health article:

> Mushrooms have been used in China for thousands of years for medicinal purposes. The West is now aware of herbal medicines. The next class of medicines will be mushrooms. Reishi (*Ganoderma* spp) mushrooms have a strong reputation for fighting health problems. Often patients are forced into medication and surgery when there are other safe alternatives.

Dr Wilkinson also stated that: 'Laboratory studies have shown that reishi and shitake mushrooms can boost the immune system.'

Though in many parts of the world mushrooms have been valued not only as a nutritious food but also for their medicinal value, in Britain and North America, up until very recently, people have to a large extent grown up with a fear or suspicion of mushrooms. This attitude is reflected in the following sentence from a fairly recent (1996) British health book, *Foods that Harm, Foods that Heal*: 'Fungi are not renowned for their medicinal properties and in Britain they are seldom, if ever, used as folk remedies.'

It seems that in English-speaking cultures there has been a historical aversion to mushrooms, associating them with toads, snails, spiders, and even witches! The ingrained fear of mushrooms in Britain may have its roots in the times of the Druids when mushrooms were associated with magic and could only be eaten under the control of the Druids themselves.

---

[27] 'Mushrooms: the new medicine' by Georgina Kenyon. BBC News, Health. 19 December 2001.

In fact, it seems that in Western culture there are generally two contrasting categories with regard to the attitude towards mushrooms. There are those people who are mycophobic, who despise mushrooms, regarding them as poisonous and associating them with evil, and those who are mycophilic and regard the mushroom as the epitome of the ultimate food.

Down through the ages mushrooms have been regarded as very special indeed. According to hieroglyphs dating back 4 600 years, the ancient Egyptians believed that mushrooms were the 'plant of immortality'. The Chinese viewed them as 'the elixir of life', and to the ancient Romans they were 'the food of the Gods'.

Interestingly, the ancient Aztecs referred to one sacramental mushroom as 'Teonance-tl', which also means 'the food of the Gods'. And more than two thousand years ago, the Greek physician Dioscurides knew that the larch polypore (*Fomitopsis officinalis*) was effective against 'consumption', the disease that is today known as tuberculosis.

The astonishing discovery of the now famous 'Iceman' in the Italian Alps, believed to have died some 5 300 years ago, brings further evidence of ancient medicinal use of mushrooms. Two pieces of birch fungus were found with the Iceman, which had been drilled through the middle and threaded on to fur strips. Birch fungus contains an antibiotic substance called polyporic acid C that is said to be highly effective against tuberculosis. These bracket fungi are also known for their properties in treating wounds, as well as stimulating the immune system. Indeed, scientists who investigated the Iceman believe that he carried the threaded birch fungus as a travelling 'medicine kit'.

But why were the Knysna elephants eating the medicinal mushroom? As I continued my research into this subject, I gradually learnt that it is probable that they consumed them for a variety of health maintenance reasons.

In the West we have seemingly created a dividing line between medicine and food, separating the one from the other. Why we have done this, I do not know. The reality, though, is that food *is* medicine.

Or to be more specific, foods contain the very elements with which we can maintain our health. The health mantra of Hippocrates back in c400BC was 'Let food be your medicine and medicine be your food'. Today, more and more people worldwide are relearning the wisdom of this truism; the right foods fuel our health.

We literally are what we eat or, rather, the recipients of the compounds of what we eat. If we eat a balanced healthy diet, it should not come as a big surprise that in turn we are more likely to be healthy individuals.

Up until very recently many of us seemed to assume that despite eating fairly healthily, drugs alone were essential to overcoming illness. Fortunately, though, more and more people are realising that diet is not only essential to optimal health, but also to the prevention of illness. An old Chinese proverb, 'medicine and food have a common origin', emphasises this fact.

The Knysna elephants were living Hippocrates's mantra of 'Let food be your medicine and medicine be your food'. I was to find *Ganoderma* in more than 50 per cent of all the dung samples I analysed over a two and a half year period. Clearly, therefore, it is very important to the Knysna elephants, despite the fact that it appears not to be eaten by elephants in other areas. Knysna elephants must therefore be consuming *Ganoderma* for a very specific and important need.

Although there has not been extensive research on *Ganoderma applanatum* (compared with *Ganoderma lucidum*, commonly known as reishi, which is today successfully artificially cultivated for commercial purposes), it has been revealed that their medicinal properties include antiviral, antibacterial, anti-parasitic effects, liver protection, and immunomodulating properties. Certain herbalists believe that *Ganoderma applanatum* and *Ganoderma lucidum* can be used more or less interchangeably. Research on *Ganoderma lucidum,* or reishi, has revealed that it contains a number of active agents that are known to modulate the immune system. The main agents are polysaccharides, triterpene compounds, sterols, coumarin and mannitols.

In Chinese herbalism, the most valued medicine is the one that has the widest spectrum of effect, and this is why the immune boosting reishi is so highly regarded. This viewpoint is the opposite of how Western doctors generally see drugs. Western doctors tend to seek specific drugs for specific ailments, concentrating on the specific symptoms, and not the body as a whole.

By contrast, in Chinese herbalism, the inferior herb or medicine is the one that acts against a specific problem. The Chinese view *Ganoderma* as an important tonic because it boosts the vital life force they call 'qi' (chi). Reishi is also highly regarded for its liver protective properties and is prescribed in China for the treatment of chronic and acute hepatitis.

By this time I had established contact with Margaret Tagwira, a biotechnology researcher and chief laboratory technician at the Africa University in Zimbabwe. Margaret had successfully domesticated a local variety of reishi (*Ganoderma lucidum*). Working with AIDS orphans, she was planning to farm the domesticated reishi commercially with the aim not only of enabling the orphans to enhance their immune systems, but also so that they could sell the reishi as a means of supporting their families.

When I first contacted Margaret, she was in the fourth year of her developmental work with medicinal mycology and the AIDS orphans. The AIDS orphans participating in Margaret's project were caring for their younger siblings, and were the heads of their parent-less households.

Appallingly and tragically, it has been estimated that Zimbabwe could have more than 900 000 AIDS orphans. At the 15th Aids Conference in Bangkok (July 2004) it was stated that by 2010 there could be more than 18 million AIDS orphans in sub-Saharan Africa.

Could *Ganoderma* play a role in the management of AIDS in Africa in the near future? It seems that indeed it could.

I learnt that medical scientists in Africa were proposing, as Margaret had, that rural people cultivate medicinal mushrooms. In 2001, for example, scientists in Tanzania were advocating that *Ganoderma* be cultivated for use as a supplement in the battle against AIDS.[28] Dr Titus Kabalimu of the Tanzania Commission for Science and Technology (Costech) said at the time:

> (Medicinal mushrooms) are not specifically active against the HIV virus in terms of killing or immobilising the virus, but it enhances body immunity to such an extent that it cures cancer pains more than any artificial analgesic. *Ganoderma lucidum* is basically a nutraceutical. It is a dietary supplement, which has medicinal functions, attributed to synergistic effects of lectins, terpenoids, steroids, nucleic acid and immunomodulatory proteins. It is advocated (that *Ganoderma*) be cultivated as a supplement to act against HIV/AIDS and TB. This mushroom does not need extraction to pure drug, but rather it is the derivatives from the fruiting body which have the proven anti-HIV/AIDS and anti-cancer properties.

---

[28] Zephania Ubwani, Mushrooms to be used in AIDS management in Tanzania. *The East African*, 8 January 2002.

An astounding photograph taken by Hylton Herd of a Knysna elephant feeding on the edge of the forest, November 2008 (Hylton Herd, SANParks)

Strangefoot, photographed for the first time by forest guard Wilfred Oraai

Strangefoot's unusual
footprints (Gareth Patterson)

Log loader of the type attacked by a musth bull (Gareth Patterson)

Forest warning sign showing damage inflicted by a musth bull (Stewart Patterson)

Knysna elephants are not confined to the forest, but frequently range in the mountain fynbos (Hylton Herd, SANParks)

Collecting samples for the DNA population study (Stewart Patterson)

Medicinal mushroom *Ganoderma applanatum* fruiting bodies on an old ironwood tree (Dominique Diane)

Stills from the 2009 documentary *The Search for the Knysna Elephants* (NHU Africa). These images were captured by film-maker Mark van Wijk on the very last day after a week of filming

Recent (2008) remote camera picture of a young bull (10 to 15 years old), very likely The Youngster (Wilfred Oraai, SANParks)

Discussing elephants with forest friends, Mrs Jordaan and her son Booi (Dominique Diane)

My forest guard friends Wilfred Oraai (left) and Karel Maswatie
(Hylton Herd, SANParks)

T W E N T Y - T H R E E

The Nature of Health

. . . rainforests, amount to the most creative laboratories on earth. Less than 10 per cent of these plant species have been systematically screened for active compounds, yet half the pharmaceutical products used by humankind at the moment come from tropical vegetation.
Douglas H Chadwick
The Fate of the Elephant, 1992

It was from Margaret Tagwira that I learnt that *Ganoderma* had been used medicinally by traditional healers in Zimbabwe for hundreds of years. At that same time, I learnt from a Ugandan herbalist that traditional healers in East Africa use *Ganoderma* for its immune boosting properties. I also discovered that in West Africa mushrooms are an important part of the traditional medical practice of the Yoruba people of southern Nigeria. And I discovered that the Wapare people of Tanzania's Kilimanjaro region use *Ganoderma* as a traditional remedy against certain livestock diseases, including the eradication of parasitic worms.

It also appeared that the oldest evidence of medicinal use of mushrooms in Africa could be found in Tassili rock paintings discovered in Northern Algeria. These paintings show a dancer, most probably a shaman, covered with repetitive mushroom symbols. These rock paintings are thought to date back to at least 5000 BC. The medicinal use of mushrooms in Africa is, therefore, very ancient.

Margaret's work revealed that certain traditional healers in Zimbabwe used *Ganoderma* for medicinal purposes and this prompted her, in turn, to ask questions about its use. But whenever she asked traditional healers what they used *Ganoderma* for, the reply was always the same, 'to treat all diseases'. At first Margaret had been discouraged by this vague answer. But then she realised that what the healers were probably indicating was that *Ganoderma* was used for all diseases because of its known immune boosting properties. As with Chinese medicine, *Ganoderma* is used in Zimbabwe for its holistic health benefits.

It intrigued both Margaret and me that wherever in the world *Ganoderma* is used as medicine, it is always steeped in hot water before being drunk as a tea. Whether it was in Zimbabwe or China, the preparation of *Ganoderma* for medicinal use was identical.

Today it has been scientifically shown that the active ingredients of *Ganoderma* are water-soluble, and therefore can be extracted with hot water. But how was this known in the ancient past?

I also learnt that it is prepared in a very similar way in Russia, where it is drunk as a highly regarded tonic known, once again, for its ability to boost the immune system. Interestingly, I also learnt that *Ganoderma* was historically used in Russia to treat wounds because of its antibacterial properties. The fruiting bodies were boiled and then hammered to produce thin elastic-like fibres. This material was used as a dressing to promote the closing of wounds.

Today commercially grown *Ganoderma* is available in capsule form and in tinctures.

What were the origins of this seemingly universal knowledge about *Ganoderma*, its medicinal use, and its preparation? How was it known, in vastly different parts of the world, that *Ganoderma* had these medicinal compounds, and that they were water-soluble, and could therefore be extracted with hot water?

Commenting on this one day, Margaret said to me: 'I am still very puzzled about the medicinal origins of *Ganoderma*. It is almost as if there was a civilisation before us, one that had more scientific medical knowledge than we have even today.'

It was during the time that Margaret and I were sharing information on our findings about *Ganoderma* that I learnt that elephant droppings were used for medicinal purposes right here in the Knysna area.

When I first heard about this, I immediately wondered whether there was a connection to the *Ganoderma*. More than 50 per cent of the dung samples I had collected contained pieces of the mushroom. When I made enquiries locally about the medicinal qualities of the dung, I was told that it detoxified the body and boosted health. No one could tell me the source of the medicinal properties, only that 'elephants eat many medicines'.

I learnt that locally the elephant droppings were boiled in water, after which the liquid was strained and drunk like a tea – exactly the same way *Ganoderma* was prepared in Africa, the East and northern Europe.

The reason I thought it was *Ganoderma*'s properties at work in the dung was the fact that locally, amongst the forest guards for example, there was no knowledge (prior to my telling them) that the Knysna elephants routinely eat the medicinal *Ganoderma*. It was knowledge that had become lost in time.

One day, when I told Wilfred about the ancient and highly regarded properties of *Ganoderma applanatum*, and that the dung contained this, he nodded his head thoughtfully and said to me, 'Then it makes sense why the dung is so good for us.'

My research into the local medicinal use of elephant droppings revealed that this knowledge actually, and not surprisingly, stemmed from the original inhabitants of the southern Cape, the San. I learnt from a forestry official that periodically people from a small, isolated community living in the Outeniqua Mountains would appear at a local forestry college and enquire whether the facility had any elephant droppings. Who were these people? Why did they want elephant droppings?

I discovered that they were direct descendants of the original San that had once inhabited the entire region.

Here and there, the old ways live on. And so it was with the San descendants. These people still held knowledge of the medicinal value contained within elephant droppings, and it was my hypothesis that the *Ganoderma* present in the dung was, in part, the source of the medicinal properties sought by the San descendants of modern times.

It is not inconceivable that Africa's *Ganoderma* species might be an even more powerful promoter of human health than the well-known reishi cultivated and exported in the East.

At the moment this is simply not known, but what if it was? The medical implications of this would be enormous. With future research into Africa's medicinal mushrooms, we might unlock solutions to some of the diseases that massively affect the continent, such as AIDS. This is not impossible. One has to remember that the very first antibiotic was a fungus, namely penicillin, the *Penicillium notatum* fungus, and that it continues to provide an effective global treatment of bacterial infections in humans.

Common infections that are treated successfully today were often deadly killers just fifty short years ago. What is not widely known, though, is that the discovery of penicillin was the relearning of ancient indigenous knowledge. It was subsequently discovered that more than three thousand years ago the Chinese covered open wounds with mouldy soybean curd to promote and speed up the healing process.

My research into *Ganoderma* led to the finding that the United Nations Development Programme (UNDP) has created a hugely important platform for research on Africa's *Ganoderma* species and their cultivation. I learnt that it was a Tanzanian, Professor Keto Mshigeni, based at the University of Namibia, who headed up this work. I contacted Keto and we exchanged information about our studies.

Keto told me that because of the knowledge of the immunoboosting properties of *Ganoderma*, the UNDP-funded project, which is

160

in partnership with Africa's relevant government ministries, is undertaking clinical testing trials of *Ganoderma* nutraceuticals with people with HIV/AIDS. The preliminary results reported so far, Keto told me, were promising.

Keto was fascinated to hear about my findings of the Knysna elephants' utilisation of *Ganoderma*, and later wrote the following about this in the science journal, *Discovery and Innovation*:

> There is a growing body of scientific knowledge supporting the notion that *Ganoderma*'s natural products display a strong medicinal potency against many ailments. It is reported to be an anti-tumour, antiviral, antibacterial, anti-parasitic, etc. It is documented to be effective as an anti-inflammatory, as a kidney tonic, as a hepatoprotective, and also as a blood pressure regulator. Additionally, it is reported to be effective in boosting the body's immunoresponse system. Thus Gareth Patterson's hypothesis that the routine consumption of *Ganoderma* mushrooms by the Knysna elephants might be a case of self-medication/health maintenance seems plausible. Verification of that hypothesis calls for collaborative research amongst wildlife scientists, mushroom scientists, and medical practitioners.

> In that regard, considering the reported immunoboosting attributes of the *Ganoderma* mushroom natural products, the Namibia-based UNDP-funded Regional Project has initiated collaborative regional research and development, under the scientific leadership of Africa's senior medical practitioners, which involves clinical testing trials of *Ganoderma* nutraceuticals on people with HIV/AIDS.

> It is not inconceivable that this collaborative research initiative on the testing of *Ganoderma* nutraceuticals against HIV/AIDS may make a meaningful contribution towards finding a sustainable solution to the devastating pandemic, which is killing many millions of people in Africa.

Ganoderma lucidum has been artificially cultivated for more than two decades now. In fact, the overwhelming majority of medicinal mushrooms can be cultivated commercially, and thus the health products produced are accessible and relatively affordable. And, most importantly, here in Africa where we are so deeply afflicted by the AIDS pandemic and poverty, people can be taught how to grow these immune boosting mushrooms. It is the hope of many that this could be a tool with which African people can fight back.

It is hoped by people like Professor Mshigeni that the cultivation of these mushrooms has not only the potential to boost the immune systems of people with HIV/AIDS in rural areas, but that through farming the mushrooms commercially in these areas poverty can be reduced as well.

Of this he wrote in the editorial:

> The mushroom farming technologies developed over the years in China and other countries in East Asia . . . can be adapted for use in Africa. Indeed . . . an increasing number of African scientists have now assimilated the basic technologies involved in mushroom farming. These pioneers will continue to perfect both the science and the art of mushroom farming through training and mushroom production practice. Already some have begun to generate an impact in their respective countries. But definitely, many more scientists need to be trained, who, in turn, will train more farmers in rural communities . . . (Medicinal mushrooms) can be grown by the poor and landless . . . one does not need expensive stretches of land to farm them. If effective post-harvest crop handling and marketing strategies are developed simultaneously, we could see Africa's mushrooms becoming a strong agent towards realising our millennium goal of poverty reduction.

The fact that the Knysna elephants are eating *Ganoderma* seemingly for medicinal reasons is yet another poignant illustration of why we desperately need to protect wildlife and the remaining wild places. We can learn from the health maintenance strategies of the animals. We humans must never forget that we, too, are products of the wilds. It is no coincidence that a massive natural pharmacy which offers healing exists in the wilds.

There are, of course, a great many other reasons why it is essential for us to protect the wilds; in the first instance it is the biodiversity of life upon which our own existence depends. And we should also protect and cherish wildlife and wild places for their intrinsic value. Now, as the science of Zoopharmacognosy emerges, it is imperative that we protect and cherish the last vestiges of our wild roots for another critical reason: therein lies the potential for curing our physical and mental ills. If we can do this (even for what could be interpreted as self-serving reasons – our own health), spiritual empathy for the wilds will, I believe, follow. What you have empathy for, you certainly will not harm.

If the last Knysna elephant had already died, neither I nor anyone else would have known that these elephants seemingly self-medicate with a medicinal mushroom that will, I am convinced, be increasingly used in complementary medicine in the years ahead. It is entirely possible that research currently being undertaken on the African *Ganoderma* species, as well as other mushroom species, will unlock significant health benefits for the people of this continent and beyond.

By understanding and recognising that animals do not depend on their immune systems alone to maintain health, but actively seek out their own medicines in the wilds, we can relearn from them how to maintain our own health.

In the Summary of the Cancer Research UK report it was stated that:

> While many of these medicinal mushrooms were both medicinal and nutritious, others (like *Ganoderma*) were inedible and only used for their medicinal qualities. Therefore how these qualities were first identified will forever be a mystery . . .

In my humble opinion this might not necessarily be so. Knowledge of the medicinal qualities of these mushrooms could have been learnt from animals . . .

Stretching back to antiquity, it is entirely possible that our very earliest knowledge of medicine was derived from our observations of how the animals around us treated their own ills – just as I observed that the Knysna elephants seemed to be self-medicating by eating the *Ganoderma*.

Today, we urgently and increasingly need to focus more and more on research into the self-medication wisdom of wildlife. In addition, if we can discover how wildlife maintains health, we will also learn about the health of the ecosystems, or rather learn that if we do not continue to devastate ecosystems, their health will return once more.

And with this, our own health will benefit immensely. We will have cleaner air, less pollution, cleaner water, greater green areas, cleaner oceans, fewer emissions. The list is endless.

Studying the self-medication wisdom of wildlife is probably one of the most important areas of wildlife research that needs to be undertaken today. We need to get out there and, humbly, watch and learn from the animals.

Through this we might also, hopefully, relearn our interconnectedness with all other life. In this process we might rid ourselves of the false, often damaging perception that human beings are apart from the animals and other life forms. We might even see ourselves once again, after a very long time, reflected in the non-human life around us.

TWENTY-FOUR

Encounters with a Musth Bull

It was Christmas morning 2003, a beautiful morning, clear and quiet, and rain had refreshed the forest the night before. As I walked through the forest up towards the place where I had first encountered Strangefoot and The Youngster all those months ago, I just knew that I was going to have another encounter with elephants.

When I was walking the last stretch of indigenous forest leading to the plantation, I suddenly felt a deep resonance in the air. It was as if the forest was filled with secret, deep voices. I did not hear the voices, but rather felt the passage of their tones as they travelled through the trees and through the earth itself. Elephants were talking . . . Feeling this, my steps became lighter and slower.

I approached the place where the track leads north and where, just beyond a corner, the plantations begin. Elephants had been there just minutes before, all the signs of their presence were right in front of me. On the sandy ground I found the imprints of three different elephants. Strangefoot's was not among them, and they were certainly too large to be those of The Youngster.

A torn off, bark-stripped branch lay directly across the track. On the grassy verge of the path was a large pile of droppings. They were very fresh indeed, still warm to the touch. More droppings lay on the road ahead of me. Branches were strewn all around. I picked up one of these, a wattle. There was moisture on the pale exposed wood, where great molars had ground down. Elephant saliva.

The elephants were all around me. They were standing motionless in the forest, probably not more than 15 or 20 metres away. It was incredible.

I could not see them, and I could not now even sense the vibration of their talk, yet I could feel their presence. The still warm droppings and chewed branches still wet with saliva, these things had betrayed their presence, but something else told me they were nearby, listening to me. It was the silence of elephants.

I stayed there for just a few minutes before moving on. No one could have given me a greater present than the one I had just received that Christmas morning in the forest.

The elephants would have detected my footfalls on the track and have signalled their infrasonic warning, which was what I had felt in the air as I approached. They would then have slipped noiselessly into the foliage.

Silently, at least to my ears, one of elephants would have rumbled the 'stand still' command. In bush lands I have seen entire herds freeze, pausing in whatever they were doing. Some would stand stock-still with a foot raised off the ground. This is 'elephant freeze frame'.

Normally, after pausing, the herd matriarch will rumble 'let's go!' and then the entire herd will rush away, some of them trumpeting, even screaming if they suspect that great danger might be near. But the Knysna elephants have little fear of humans. In the forest, they have the advantage of cover, and they know our human ways well. When detecting the presence of humans they slip silently into the vast greenery, and remain motionless until the people, be they on foot, bicycle, car or truck, have passed by. Then the elephants might even step back on to the track and resume their feeding. As though nothing had happened.

In all likelihood this would have happened after I moved away, and I wondered, 'Which elephants were these?'

The tracks had not been those of Strangefoot, nor did I think they were those of The Youngster. They were large, as were the balls of dung. One of the elephants might have been the young adult cow Wilfred and Karel had come across fast asleep in the Maraisbos. Another might have been the Young Bull sighted and photographed by Wilfred back in 2000. But of the third elephant, I had no idea.

Knowing how things work here, though, I would not have been surprised if the tracks belonged to other 'previously unknown' Knysna elephants.

Ten days into the New Year, I had quite a different encounter with a Knysna elephant. I was walking in particularly dense vegetation when I came across very fresh feeding signs and droppings. But on this occasion, there was another factor at work. I detected a strong, acrid smell and immediately, without knowing why, I knew I had to get away from the place. Fast. It was as if my mind was exploding with warning signals.

'GO, GO, GO!'

As I quickly moved away, I heard a loud movement down in a small valley to my left. Out of sight, and veiled by a wall of trees and scrub, was an elephant.

I did not pause to try to see the elephant. I was filled with what I can only describe as a deeply ominous feeling, as though my life was in great danger.

What was the reason for the extreme urgency to move away?

And what was that pungent smell?

Two days later, forester Dominique du Toit was driving along Kom se Pad towards Diepwalle forest station, where she works. As she turned a corner, she saw that trees had been knocked down and that earth had been gouged out of an embankment.

Then she heard an elephant just out sight in the forest, as it slammed yet another tree to the ground. The ground shook, and Dominique shivered.

'It all seemed very destructive. There was such aggression in the air,' she told me a few days later when she recounted what she had witnessed that morning on Kom se Pad.

She had unconsciously sensed the testosterone that had been raging.

Dominique drove on quickly, and when she reached the forest station she told Wilfred what she had seen. Wilfred set out to investigate, walking silently on Kom se Pad. After a while he too heard the elephant. It was clearly ahead of him, and most likely right on the road itself.

When he heard the sounds, Wilfred knew that something unusual was going on. In all his years of experience, he had never known a Knysna elephant to make such a noise from afar in the forest. These were normally elephants of quietness.

Why is this one making such noise? Wilfred wondered, as he moved forward.

A chill of trepidation suddenly swept over him . . .

The elephant came into view. It was standing on the side of the track, and at first Wilfred could only see its hindquarters. Then it turned. Wilfred saw both sides of his head were streaked with dark liquid, copious fluid from the temporal glands. The wind suddenly shifted and Wilfred almost recoiled from the strong smell delivered from the direction of the bull elephant. Then Wilfred saw the bull's penis. Urine was dribbling from the organ. The insides of the bull's hind legs were soaked black by the wetness. Wilfred had never seen an elephant like this before.

Back in 1977, Joyce Poole had witnessed an Amboseli bull elephant in a similar condition. Initially she did not know what was wrong with the bull. She wrote in her field notes:

> The constant dribbling of urine had apparently caused the sheath of his penis to turn a greenish colour from what seemed to be a nasty fungal growth . . . Studying the male . . . I estimated that he must be at least fifty years old. Perhaps old elephants become incontinent . . .'

But Joyce was to discover that this condition was much more than an old bull with incontinence. She later read a paper about how Asian bull elephants, on reaching adulthood, come into a condition known as musth.

Musth is a Hindi term that means 'intoxicated' and describes the testosterone-charged condition that bulls come into periodically. It is a time of intense sexual and aggressive activity. Depending on the hierarchical rank of the bull, it can persist for months. Learning this, everything fell into place for Joyce.

She made the dramatic discovery that African elephants also come into musth, something that had not previously been known to science. Behavioural studies of African animals is relatively young. Iain Douglas-Hamilton can be considered one of the early pioneers of elephant behaviour with his study of the Manyara elephants in the 1960s. The relative youthfulness of this science, less than the lifetime of a human, puts into perspective how little we actually know about African wildlife.

Joyce went on to undertake a two-year study into the musth phenomenon of male elephants. It was a time often fraught with danger, given the aggressiveness the bulls commonly display when in this condition.

'No animal in the world is as dangerous as an elephant in musth,' wrote Charles Darwin of Asian bull elephants.

One Amboseli bull in particular, 'Bad Bull', almost cost Joyce her life on several occasions. Fellow elephant expert and researcher, Cynthia Moss, described these times:

> Bad Bull . . . gave Joyce a very bad time. She was extremely frightened at first and came back to camp white-faced and shaken on many occasions, but Joyce is one of the most determined people I know and she continued to go out with the elephants . . .

The following is Joyce's own description of her encounters with musth bulls:

> During the first few months of my study, I often erred in judgement as I followed a musth male too closely . . . at the time I was still a relative novice at discerning the moods of elephants, and on many occasions my own miscalculations brought me dangerously close to death . . . suddenly the bull swung around and came for me, his ears folded under, his head and trunk down . . . he meant to tusk the car!
> . . . I was about to be killed! I drove through the gap as he came for me . . . with only a few feet to spare.

On another occasion:

> I knew that Bad Bull would attack before my observation period was over, and I knew that I had to be ready. But, as always, he caught me by surprise . . . he attacked . . . I put the car in second gear, and stalled. By the time I started the car again and got it moving, I could see his tusks in the rear view mirror only centimetres from the back window. Again I floored the accelerator . . . Mature male elephants can move at a good forty kilometres per hour, and the . . . (vehicle) couldn't do much more than that at the best of times. I'll never know quite how I escaped.

I, too, had experienced the aggressive behaviour of musth bulls. In the Tuli bushlands one day a bull that I knew to be normally placid, suddenly turned and, with his head down, stormed at my vehicle. Initially I shouted at the bull, as I would when being mock-charged by an elephant. Within a second, though, I understood that this was no mock charge. This bull was fuelled with intent, ignited by the testosterone racing within him. The bull meant to hit the Land Rover. I gunned the vehicle and drove away.

On another occasion I was passing a big bull, when suddenly I saw him spin around (and, make no mistake, despite their great bulk, elephants can indeed spin around), then wickedly he tusked a low mopane tree. After this, he pounded towards me and I accelerated away. He pursued me for almost a kilometre. When in musth, bull elephants turn from Dr Jekyll into Mr Hyde.

That morning in the forest Wilfred watched as the Knysna bull aggressively tusked yet another tree. Then, without thinking, Wilfred quickly slipped into the green gloom of the forest beyond the verge of the road. Something had told him urgently to get out of sight. And there, crouched amongst ferns and towering trees, he felt more secure, hidden.

A few minutes later, the bull pulled himself up on to the embankment on the side of the road, and made his way up towards the slopes of the Jonkersberg. Wilfred waited a little while before he emerged from his hiding place. The raging bull, though, was to have the last say that morning.

Just as Wilfred stepped lightly back on to the road, there was an almighty crash. The ground shook. Forest birds cried, and then flew rapidly from their perches. The urgent flapping of their wings rattled sharply like a volley of shots.

The bull had slammed yet another tree to the ground.

A few days later Wilfred told me about his encounter with the musth bull. As he was speaking, things fell into place in my own mind. Several times he mentioned the strong smell in the vicinity of the elephant. It was the same strange scent I had smelt two days earlier.

Within two days we had both encountered the musth bull.

As Wilfred spoke, I realised that if I had not moved away when I had, things could have worked out quite differently. I could have been killed. And two days later Wilfred could also have been killed if the same bull had sensed his presence.

I told Wilfred that from his descriptions, the smell, the constant dribbling of urine, the black wetness on the inside of the hind legs, all of these signs indicated that he had come across a bull in musth.

We spoke about this for some time. I told him how aggressive bull elephants can be in this condition, and that they can be in musth for months. I also told him that should he come across any signs of an elephant again in that condition, he should not attempt to track it.

I know that neither Wilfred nor I would ever forget the strange pungent smell of the musth bull. And in this was a lesson for both of us. When I picked up the scent, I immediately knew I had to move away, but I had not known why.

I had made no conscious connection between the smell and the presence of a musth bull, nor did I have to. Something else had told me urgently that I had to leave quickly. This, I understood only later, was the unconscious at work.

A week or so later, I suddenly remembered something that scientist and author Lyall Watson had once written about smell. It was a subject that he had researched extensively and had written about in his book *Jacobson's Organ*. This was to unlock an understanding of what had occurred that day when I encountered the musth bull. I had experienced that morning an extraordinary chemical warning that possibly had saved my life.

Lyall had written the following:

> Important smells, the ones that change our lives, seem to get imprinted somewhere deep in the brain in a form that gives them extraordinary clarity . . . Smell is an emotional sense rather than an intellectual one. It is more right-brain than left-brain, more

intuitive than logical, and therefore more likely to be unconsciously than consciously perceived. All of which appears to make odour-linked memories almost impossible to forget. They come to us, more often than not, via the Jacobson's organ and constitute a vital protection system, making it possible for us to learn, often in one short trial, that something is dangerous and needs to be avoided in the future . . .

Locked within me was the memory of the scent of musth bulls I have encountered in the past. This had been neatly filed away for future use. And that morning with the Knysna bull in musth, the memory of the scent had come to the forefront, telling my conscious self that I was in danger and had to get away.

I contacted Lyall Watson and described my experience with the musth bull to him.

He commented as follows:

> Thinking about elephants in musth, I am sure you are right about the smell as a warning signal, even to other species. I have seen a bull in this condition using the tip of his trunk to smear the substance from the temporal gland all over himself and his surroundings. So within the species, the odour is both an attractant and a warning – and I see no reason why such emissions should not double as interspecific warnings. Evolution never wastes such useful multi-purpose signals and substances. Co-specific females most easily detect musth in most mammals. Human males are relatively insensitive to it, but that is certainly not true of humans of either sex when walking out in the wild. The uneasiness many of us feel in the vicinity of even an invisible bull elephant in musth is, I feel certain, the result of a phenomenal component in the secretion that produces a rush of adrenalin in our systems when detected by someone like you or me or a cautious forester. A rush that results in prudent and immediate flight.

TWENTY-FIVE

The Old Man and the Matriarch

Thirty-nine years ago, a man set out on a task much like my own. For a year and three months, he walked the forests and learnt of the ways and numbers of the Knysna elephants. This was the very first time that an extensive study had been undertaken to determine the true status of the Knysna elephants. Back at that time, they often roamed the forests and the fynbos close to the coast in the Harkerville area.

The man was Nick Carter, a bush-wise former East African game warden. At the outset of the study, Carter had been warned that the Knysna elephants were dangerous and vicious. But at the conclusion of his study he stated that the elephants' reputation was completely unfounded; it was a case of 'give a dog a bad name and hang him', and that 'I have never come across such a civilised group of elephants in all my career'.

Carter gave identity and personality to the Knysna elephants. Before his study, they were generally perceived locally as creatures to be feared. At the time, there was much ignorance and misunderstanding about the Knysna elephants. Fuelled with this fear, people who lived on smallholdings adjacent to the Harkerville forests would fire their guns at night if they thought an elephant was nearby. They would shoot at shadows, which often turned out to be elephants.

Carter was certain that these indiscriminate shootings resulted in the deaths of a number of elephants. Wounded elephants would have succumbed to their injuries in deep valleys and other lonely places, and no one would even have known that they had died. The situation infuriated and frustrated Carter. Checks and counters simply did not exist to curb the indiscriminate and irresponsible firing of guns by the people living on the smallholdings.

Carter came to know well a large bull elephant that routinely moved south from the central forest to the Harkerville forests abutting the cliffs and coves on the ocean's edge. In doing so, the elephant would cross an area known locally as the 'The Garden of Eden', and Carter fittingly named this bull Adam.[29] I think Carter loved this elephant very much.

According to Carter, Adam was 'an even tempered animal, completely blasé of human sounds and activity'.

But one day a senior forestry official secretly ordered that Adam be killed. A German-born forester and hunter did the deed, and did it badly. Adam was wounded, and the hunter ran away. Adam suffered for two days with three bullets in his head, before the hunter finally returned and killed him. The killing had been done 'in secret' to prevent 'embarrassment to the forestry department'.

When Adam's body was discovered, a press release was issued by the very same forestry official who had ordered the elephant's killing. The press release stated that the elephant had died of natural causes and that the tusks had 'probably been stolen by Coloured honey hunters'.

The truth, however, inevitably came to light and a huge public scandal ensued. The killing of Adam grabbed the headlines nationally and internationally, and virtually every newspaper in the country covered the story. The killer and the person who ordered the killing were arrested and charged, but later in court the men were acquitted on a simple technicality. In disgrace, both men subsequently left the area.

Even before the killing of Adam, Carter had suspected that certain

---

[29] Adam, Carter concluded during the study, was the very same bull known as 'Aftand' ('broken tooth') by the local people and the forestry department.

forestry officials, among others, might have been involved in the killing of Knysna elephants, and that such killings were the reason why the elephant numbers had not increased over the years.

He wrote the following about this in one of his reports:

> The main reason that the elephant numbers have not increased since the last officially approved hunting of them by Major Pretorius in 1920, is that they have been killed illegally. It has been proved beyond doubt in other countries and continents that protection is not afforded merely by declaring animals to be 'Royal Game' or something similar. Physical protection has to be provided on the ground in the shape of game wardens and their staff. There appears to be nothing of that sort in the Knysna Forests. The elephants roam on land owned or administered by different sets of people: private farmers, timber companies and state forests. None of the bodies is responsible officially for the protection of the animals . . .

In the same report, Carter cites evidence of the elephant killings:

> Lest it be thought that this is mere speculation, I add that the bull, Adam, shows an unmistakable bullet hole in the top centre of his left ear and a scar on his belly, and I conclude that these might have been made by one of the light calibre rifles with which the area is infested. I have . . . evidence of the shooting of four elephants . . . and . . . found the bones of a half grown animal that had been shot in the depths of Gouna main forest. Personally I have no doubt that others have been shot more recently. They are also in danger from the desultory shooting of farmers who discharge their pieces in the general direction of any noise in the night.

In her wonderful book *The Knysna Elephants and their Forest Home* (1996), Margo Mackay echoed Carter's view that forestry officials might have been involved in the deaths of Knysna elephants. When compiling her book, Margo spoke to many people associated with the forest to try to understand what had caused the decline in Knysna elephant numbers. The opinions of these people fell into the following categories:

- Sniping by smallholders, the wounds eventually proving fatal.
- Poaching by forestry officials who had the knowledge and the opportunity to get away with it.
- The elephants, or some of them, are still there, hidden away in remoter areas.

When Carter completed his year-long study, he had identified and counted eleven elephants in the Harkerville forests. In his final report on his findings, he urged that a game reserve be established for the elephants in the Harkerville forests. The Knysna elephants needed urgent protection. He stated: 'The slenderness of a thread by which this little group of elephants hangs on to its existence must be emphasised. The urgency for conservation measures must be stressed.'

But Carter's report and findings were ignored by the authorities. Of this he wrote once:

> . . . my findings burst upon the world with all of the effect of a poached egg hitting the Indian Ocean. (The authorities) pooh-poohed most of my report and stated . . . that the forests were capable of supporting only a . . . handful of elephants.

Having been a game warden in East Africa, Carter knew elephants, but the authorities did not and later, after the killing of Adam, the subject of the elephants was an embarrassment to the forestry department. Understanding this, Carter knew that the future of the Knysna elephants could not be left to authority alone.

'Officialdom will do nothing unless it is badgered continuously, starting from now,' he wrote angrily in 1974.

Carter held great and understandable concern for the elephants:

> . . . if nothing is done, one day some of our children may look up from a book and say: 'Whatever happened to the Knysna elephants?'

Quite suddenly, in 1977, the Knysna elephants became completely absent from the Harkerville forest, which was very strange indeed.

This had, after all, been the main area in which Carter had encountered the elephants during his study in 1969-1970. The elephants had been utilising this area regularly for some fifteen years, according to some records. In Carter's year-long study, the Knysna elephants had almost always utilised the Harkerville forest:

> . . . I can state with absolute certainty that there have only been two periods of a week and two weeks respectively, when the Harkerville forest had been empty of elephants during the past year.

For the elephants to leave, great tragedy and equally great trauma must have occurred. We do not know what happened in this place previously much favoured by the elephants. But perhaps the smallholders, or certain former forestry officials, do. Something horrendous took place in the Harkerville forest that made Knysna elephants flee. Margo Mackay wrote in her book :

> Up until as recently as 1977, members of the herd trekked in spring to the sweeter veld of the Harkerville Coastal Forest and back again to the Diepwalle/Gouna Forest for winter. Suddenly this trek ceased and the elephants were seen no more in the Harkerville Forest. It is reasonable to suppose that harassment was the prime cause of this change of pattern.

The lack of protection or concern for the Knysna elephants was to plague and frustrate Nick Carter for much of the rest of his life. He remained in the Knysna area after his elephant study, settling there with his wife Gillian. He wrote a book on the elephants of Knysna and remained resolute, an ally and strong spokesperson for these unique elephants.

Future generations will owe much to the important emphasis Nick Carter put upon the Knysna elephants.

In 2004, Nick Carter passed away. He was eighty-six years old. We never met, as he had been ill for a number of years. He suffered from Alzheimer's disease, a disease that affects parts of the brain that control thought, memory and language. It seems that with this disease, nerve cells die in areas of the brain that are vital to memory and other mental abilities. There is no cure and the disease becomes progressively worse.

During his last years, this disease erased from Nick Carter's mind his connection with the elephants of Knysna. Or so it seemed.

His wife Gillian is a friend of mine. Over the past years, I have regularly given Gillian updates on my findings.

A short time before he died, Nick one day suddenly appeared to be completely lucid. And during that brief window of lucidity he said to Gillian, 'This man you speak of, Gareth, the man who is studying the Knysna elephants, do you trust him? Is he a good man?'

'Yes, Nick,' Gillian replied, greatly surprised by the question and the apparent clarity of his thoughts.

'That's good then,' Nick mused.

The elephants had never been far from his mind, not even right towards the end.

'Where is the Matriarch?' This question had puzzled me during the first three years of my study of the Knysna elephants. At the onset of the study, Wilfred and Karel had not seen any sign of her for almost two years. For almost half a decade she had been absent from her old haunts in the vicinity of the Diepwalle forest station and Kom se Pad. The guards and I presumed, sadly, that she was dead. After the capture of the Kruger orphans in 1999, she simply disappeared . . .

The Matriarch was elsewhere. In places where elephants had not roamed for almost a quarter of a century.

Tragically, as I was completing the writing of this book, Lyall Watson passed away. Lyall Watson was a man who had made the mysterious the mission of his life. *Supernature, Gifts of Unknown Things, Lifetide* and, most recently, *Elephantoms* are but a few of his well-known books.

Lyall wrote about 'the soft edges of science', of things otherwise not understood or explained. In his book *Heaven's Breath* he even wrote a natural history of the wind, a riveting read about the intangible, the air.

Lyall had an almost magical connection with the Knysna elephants and the forests. It was here as a child, more than half a century ago, that Lyall saw the secret elephants for the first time.

Lyall visited me one day in 2003, and together we walked the forest. He told me that he had returned here in the year of the new millennium and that he had witnessed a most remarkable thing. One day he had walked the coves and beaches where he had spent childhood holidays, the shoreline that borders on the Harkerville forest. After walking for some hours, he sat down on a high cliff overlooking the ocean. As he sat there he suddenly saw the largest animal the world has ever known, a blue whale. Lyall immediately stood up, marvelling at the sight.

Then he felt a strange throbbing in the air.

He turned and looked across a gorge, and saw an elephant facing towards the sea. It was the Matriarch! There she was! After almost a quarter of a century she had reclaimed the Harkerville forests. Unseen, she had silently been roaming Nick Carter's old stamping ground.

Whatever had driven the elephants from this place had now, happily, passed. The ancient elephant pathways at Harkerville had beckoned again and the Matriarch had heard the call.

She had returned, and as Lyall watched her that day, the old cow elephant listened to another ancient song. Like her own kind, blue whales communicate by infrasound. It was as though the largest animal of the ocean and the largest land animal were conversing with each other. Lyall wrote about this in his book *Elephantoms*:

> The Matriarch was here for the whale . . . they were no more than a
> hundred yards apart and I was convinced they were communicating

. . . woman to woman, matriarch to matriarch, almost the last of their kind.

I turned, blinking away the tears, and left them to it. This was no place for a mere man . . .

TWENTY-SIX

Discovering Elephants by DNA

During the first three years of the study, I had several glimpses of the Knysna elephants, or rather, I had seen fragments of them. I had seen patches of dark flanks at the Secret Place, flashes of grey shadows in the plantations, and dark movements in dense forest. Each of these almost magical 'sightings' left me feeling enthralled and deeply moved.

Then in May 2004, I had my first full view sighting of a Knysna elephant. This lasted four or five seconds at the very most. One winter's morning while investigating an area north of the Steenbras River, which I had discovered was visited fairly frequently by the elephants, I came across fresh feeding signs and spoor.

I leant over and examined a large creased oval imprinted on a patch of disturbed soil. Then I looked ahead of me down a faint track. And there it was. Some fifty metres away a young elephant was soundlessly crossing the track. Its head was raised as it walked, and was turned in my direction. Clearly, the elephant was aware of my presence, but was not unduly alarmed, just watchful, cautious, almost curious. I estimated that the elephant was about six to seven years old, and assumed that its mother had crossed the track just seconds before. Though I could not be certain from such a brief sighting, I thought this elephant was female.

I remained unmoving as the elephant dissolved into dense vegetation. I listened. Minutes passed, then I heard brushing movements to my right, perhaps thirty metres away. I stepped back several paces, then turned and walked away.

I was stunned by what I had seen. To see a Knysna elephant, in full view, even if only for a few seconds, is an extraordinary experience.

Several months later I saw this young elephant again, at least I presume it was the same one. On this occasion, I saw the mother too. Fransje was with me when this sighting took place. One afternoon we were walking in some high country that overlooked open harvested plantation areas, interspersed with stands of pines. I had been scanning the land far below us with my binoculars when suddenly I saw the elephants. I took the binoculars from my eyes and stared below, amazed once again at what I had seen. I raised the binoculars again and saw an adult female, even the glint of her tusks in the sunlight. And beside her, a little to the right, was the youngster.

We stayed on the rise for almost an hour, peering below with the binoculars, both of us quite enthralled at what we were seeing. Then the elephants slowly moved off; the deepening shadows, almost possessively, engulfed them and they were no longer visible. The door had been opened for us and we had looked in. Then the door had slowly, almost inevitably, closed and it was over. Almost like a dream.

This sighting somehow marked the end of the innocence of the study. The seemingly endless days of discovery, learning about the elephants from signs and interpretations in the forest and mountains were about to change. This was not a bad thing; quite the opposite. I was entering a new phase of the study, a phase that would, importantly, reveal the number, sexes and degree of relatedness of the Knysna elephants, vital information to be harnessed, with the diet and range findings, for the long-term preservation of the secret elephants, the flagship species for all the other animals of this special region.

Lori Eggert is an American conservation geneticist whose principal research focuses on non-invasive means of providing information for the effective management of declining species, secretive or dangerous animals in general, and elephants in particular. Her PhD research dealt with the conservation of the African forest elephant and the evolutionary relationships between forest and savannah elephant populations across west and central Africa. During this research, she developed a genetic censusing method for forest elephants using DNA extracted from dung samples.

Determining elephant numbers and population structures in forest environments has always been notoriously difficult. As I knew only too well in the forests, mountain fynbos and plantations in the southern Cape, dense vegetation makes sightings (and photography) of individual animals incredibly difficult, and the undertaking of direct census methods impossible. In recent years, 'dung count' census methods have been developed to estimate population numbers. This entails calculating elephant numbers by the counting of dung piles located on transects in the study area. Final population estimates are corrected by the inclusion of variables such as decomposition of dung piles, decay rates and other factors such as rainfall. This innovative indirect method of censusing forest elephants, despite the questioning of its accuracy by some scientists, has produced very impressive results, and according to Richard Barnes, the chief protagonist of this method, provides population size estimates as precise as any other method used for a wide range of animals.

Dung density data, though, cannot tell us about the sex ratio or the degree of relatedness between individual elephants. Also the dung count method cannot tell us about the genetic diversity present in the population, which is so important in assessing the long-term survival of a potentially inbred elephant population. This is where Lori Eggert's groundbreaking DNA work comes in and complements significantly the means required for a greater understanding of forest elephants and a myriad of other secretive and elusive animals.

Lori and her research colleagues conducted a groundbreaking genetic survey of forest elephants in the Kakum National Park in Ghana. Little was known about Kakum's elephants. The area is surrounded by agriculture, and whatever elephants existed were thought to be an isolated population, as no other elephants lived in the remnants of forest adjacent to the park.

Because the fibrous vegetation eaten by elephants continuously scrapes cells from the intestines, dung is a very rich source of DNA. Following the elephant paths at Kakum, Lori and her fellow researchers collected dung samples. First they measured the circumference of the sample dung bolus (ball). This was done to determine age structures of the population. The body sizes of elephants and bolus circumferences have been shown to be directly related, and hence age can be estimated. Then a portion of the dung was collected and placed in tubes with preservative for the laboratory DNA extraction procedures. In total, 205 dung samples were collected.

Extracting and analysing DNA from the faecal samples, an intensive process, revealed impressive results from the Kakum samples. Eighty-nine adult elephants were identified, as well as twenty-nine juveniles. The Kakum study provided the first estimate of numbers and demographics of a forest elephant population using genetic data extracted from dung. Collecting blood or tissue material from forest elephants to undertake such a census would have been impossible, in fact suicidal, to attempt. But Lori's non-invasive sampling techniques proved not only to be a successful means of estimating the size of a forest elephant population, but also showed how this reliable DNA censusing method can be used to study other secretive or dangerous species – population studies that previously were not possible by other means.

After learning about Lori's work I contacted her and told her about my work and findings on the Knysna elephants, and how important it was to unlock the mystery of how many Knysna elephants exist, and to conclusively uncover the demographics of the population. Because so little was known about the Knysna elephants in the past, basic facts about their ecology, habitat requirements and estimated numbers, consensus on the way forward for these elephants has been somewhat hazy and haphazard – a potentially perilous situation for this important and endangered elephant population, the most southerly elephants in the world. I knew this situation would only change if hard scientific data on the elephant's status was presented to the authorities, and to the public at large.

I outlined my work into the diet and range of the elephants to Lori, telling her that I had recorded elephant utilisation of some one hundred plant species, from forest, mountain fynbos and successional areas. I reported my findings on the elephants' consumption of the medicinal *Ganoderma*, and how they utilise a far larger (and more diverse) range than was previously known. I also told Lori of my findings on the population itself, how both the guards and I had evidence that several previously unknown young adult Knysna elephants existed, that this included at least one sexually mature bull, and that one known birth had taken place in the past three years.

Lori felt that the Knysna elephants were exactly the kind of endangered population that could potentially benefit from her genetic censusing methods. She proposed that we collaborate on a population study using this method.

We set the wheels in motion to begin the study: importation permits for the samples, permission from the state and from other landowners on whose property the Knysna elephants roam, and the welcome cooperation of forester friends and, of course, the forest guards. From Washington Lori sent me a package of sampling equipment, the polypropylene test tubes, buffer (preservative), data lists, and detailed instructions on how samples should be collected, preserved and stored prior to shipping to the USA. We aimed to collect at least thirty dung samples and, as with the study at Kakum, I would also be measuring bolus circumference during the sampling for age estimation of the elephants.

During the next four months, I collected samples in the central range of the elephants, as well as in the west beyond the Knysna River, in the Goudveld area. On several occasions when I found fresh signs it was clear that two elephants were moving together, most probably Strangefoot and The Youngster, judging from the size of the tracks. On one occasion, though, it seemed to me that three elephants were moving in the same area and, much later, when the DNA findings were completed, this was confirmed.

In total, I collected thirty-five samples, the majority of which were 'fresh' and ideal for the laboratory work. Then I packaged the sample test tubes carefully and sent them off to Lori at the Smithsonian Institution in Washington DC.

TWENTY-SEVEN

Baby Elephantom

During the months of waiting for the preliminary results of the DNA work, I resumed fieldwork on the diet and distribution of the elephants and during this time a myriad of issues and circumstances arose. I found evidence once again of a bull in musth; there was the tragic death of an elephant handler at a captive elephant tourism facility near Knysna; we discovered proof of the existence of another Knysna calf; and I found evidence that the Knysna elephants were moving again in areas from which they had been absent for decades.

It was in the first quarter of the year that reports reached me that an elephant had inflicted extensive damage, running into thousands of rands, to harvesting equipment in the commercial plantation areas. One night a parked log loader vehicle had been attacked, and one of its large tyres had been tusked. Other equipment had been barged into and tossed around.

On hearing the news, I immediately thought this might be the action of a bull in musth. It was almost exactly a year since Wilfred and I had our separate experiences with the musth bull. As mentioned earlier, the musth condition, a time of heightened levels of aggression and dominance, is cyclic, and occurs annually. Therefore, to hear of elephant damage and aggressive elephant behaviour at this time of year was not unexpected. From the study perspective, this damage to harvesting equipment, and damage that had occurred annually in the past, reinforced the evidence that a mature male was coming into musth each year.

It was interesting to note that the target of the bull's aggression, the log loaders, have somewhat elephant-like characteristics in a strange, almost Dali-esque way. At the front of these imposing vehicles is the prominent outstretched (trunk-like) crane component used for grasping and moving logs. Given the appearance of these large vehicles, it was not altogether surprising that a testosterone-fuelled bull elephant might, particularly under the cover of night, vent his aggression on parked log loaders.

Forester Len du Plessis contacted me about the elephant damage and asked whether I had any ideas how such damage could be prevented in the future. A solution, in theory, I told Len, might lie in the use of chilli pepper. For several years now in Southern and East Africa, research has been undertaken on the use of chilli as a deterrent to crop-raiding elephants. Elephants it seems, definitely have an aversion to the smell and taste of chilli. The burning of 'bricks' consisting of elephant dung mixed with chilli keeps elephants from entering croplands. Elephants are also deterred when chilli plants are grown on the perimeters of fields, and this also provides farmers with the bonus of a second cash crop.

It was at the time that Len and I were discussing plans to prevent musth bull damage to harvesting equipment that I heard of another human/elephant conflict, this time tragic and fatal. An elephant handler, Tobias Ndlovu, was killed by Harry, a young bull at the Knysna elephant park, one of two captive elephant tourism facilities in the Knysna-Plettenberg Bay area. This sad incident added to the already strong backlash in South Africa and internationally against the then largely unregulated captive elephant industry. No laws existed to govern methods used within this industry, with handlers requiring no formal training or education to 'manage' or work with captive elephants.

The elephants used in the captive elephant tourism industry are usually traumatised cull orphans, or even calves literally stolen from their family herds in the wilds. Many readers will remember the 'Tuli baby elephant scandal' when thirty young elephants were captured, snatched from their families in the Tuli bushlands, chained in captivity and subjected to cruel beatings in preparation for tourism purposes in South Africa, as well as for sale to international zoos. Such orphans are 'trained' for elephant back safaris, walks, and 'touch/hug an elephant' enterprises in South Africa and Zimbabwe. Presently it is estimated that almost one hundred wild-born elephants are used for tourism purposes in the captive elephant industry in South Africa.

Soon after the death of the handler at the elephant park a journalist asked me my thoughts on the incident and on captive elephant tourism in general. I said that though I was not present when the tragedy took place, I could say that it was a well-known fact that being an elephant handler or keeper is a very hazardous occupation – so much so that statistically it is listed as the most dangerous occupation in North America, according to the United States Bureau of Labour. I also said that I felt that wild-born elephants should not be held in captivity, and the tragedy raised the question of the future of Harry, the young bull that killed the handler.

The keeping of captive elephants is without doubt hazardous, but is doubly dangerous when it is undertaken in areas where wild elephant populations exist. Holding captive elephants where free-ranging elephants roam creates conflict situations not only for humans, but also for the elephants themselves. In Asia, wild musth bulls regularly break into captive facilities to mate with females in oestrus. Wild bulls father some eighty per cent of all calves born in captivity in countries like India. Captive bulls have been known to die during the break-ins after sustaining injuries from their wild counterparts.

Such conflict situations are now occurring in Southern Africa with the establishment of elephant-back safaris and 'walking with elephants' tourism operations. The well-known elephant bull Abu, star of many feature movies including Clint Eastwood's 'White Hunter, Black Death' as well as 'Circles in a Forest', the cinematic dramatisation of Dalene Matthee's book about the Knysna elephants and the forest woodcutter communities, died after sustaining injuries from a wild musth bull in Northern Botswana.

Tragedies such as this will continue to be repeated if, for tourism purposes, captive elephants are kept in the vicinity of wild populations in Southern Africa. Recent research in Namibia has revealed that when atmospheric conditions are optimum, bull elephants can hear female elephants' infrasonic oestrus calls throughout an area of some three hundred square kilometres – which is a huge area. The existence in the Knysna-Plettenberg Bay area of two captive elephant facilities, well within a similar sized area abutting the Knysna elephant population range, has for long been a great concern of mine. Knowing that the Knysna elephants were now increasingly ranging into historical areas from which they been absent for several decades because of human disturbance factors has, in fact, increased my concern that one day conflict might arise as a result of the positioning of the local elephant tourism operations.

In November 2004, a report reached me that tracks and other signs of a female elephant had been found in an area east of the central range of the Knysna elephants. This alone was intriguing (and, taking the above into consideration, also somewhat worrying) as it was a further indication that the elephants were once again beginning to utilise historical range. The report was also somewhat different to others I have gratefully received on signs of the presence of elephants, as it mentioned that it seemed there was also evidence of a young calf.

The bearer of this astonishing news was Tony Kinahan, co-owner of the Buffalo Hills Game Reserve, a private wildlife sanctuary some 20 kilometres east of where I live on the edge of the forest. The morning after my conversation with Tony, Fransje and I set out early to investigate. We planned to meet up with Tony and the Buffalo Hills game guides and accompany them on foot to where the signs of the elephants had been found.

We had not driven more than ten kilometres on the road up towards the Diepwalle forest station when suddenly I saw evidence of an elephant crossing the dirt track. On closer inspection, we saw that the tracks were very recent, just an hour or so old, and were those of an elephant of The Youngster's age. I backtracked the spoor and found where the elephant had emerged from the dense forest. There it had fed along the verge of the road before ambling down the side of the track for some thirty metres. Then the elephant crossed the road and entered the equally dense forest on the other side.

As these tracks were fresh, and we had found them only a two-hour walk (for an elephant) from where Tony had found tracks the day before, I immediately wondered if it was the same elephant. But the one on the road that morning, as I double-checked, was clearly alone. There was certainly no sign of a calf.

Later, on meeting up with Tony and the game guides, we set off on foot across a wide plateau towards the (aptly named) Elephant Gorge through which the Bitou River flows down towards the ocean. This area was relatively new to me but I knew that records showed that Knysna elephants had been absent from it for almost thirty years. After some twenty minutes, the guides began to scan the ground for the signs they had come across the day before. Then suddenly we saw it: depressions in the grassy vegetation and strewn wattle branches, clear evidence of elephant. Though I had not doubted Tony's report, pausing there and looking across towards the coastal town of Plettenberg Bay and the ocean, I was amazed that elephants were in this area.

We walked quietly onwards along a trail. Then I saw one of the guides point to the ground and gesture to me. There was no mistake; at his feet amongst the fynbos groundcover was a pile of little elephant droppings. This was irrefutable evidence of the existence of a Knysna calf. I was astonished and overjoyed.

The others gathered around and Fransje asked, 'How old is the baby, Gareth?' I thought the calf must be about two years old, certainly no more than that.

To be doubly sure about my estimation of the calf's age I measured the circumference of one of the dung balls and sent this information to Soila Saiyielel, an elephant research colleague of Joyce Poole's at Amboseli in Kenya. I also sent the circumference measurements to a game ranger friend of mine, Jed Bird at the Addo Elephant National Park. Both could make comparisons of the circumference measurements with calves of known age in those parks. The feedback from Soila and Jed indicated that this Knysna baby was approximately a year and a half old.

TWENTY-EIGHT

The Awakening

Free from death . . .
the free creature has its progress always behind it,
and God before it, and when it moves, it moves
in eternity, as streams do.
Rainer Maria Rilke
Duino Elegies

In April 2005, some 900 square kilometres of the Knysna elephants' rangelands were formally transferred to the custodianship of South African National Parks (SANParks). The swathes of dense indigenous forest and other lands previously managed by the forestry department were officially designated to receive National Park status in the near future. This was an enormously significant and important development for the long-term preservation of the Knysna elephants and all other animal life on the southern tip of Africa.

When the land is declared South Africa's youngest National Park,[30] a holistic approach can begin in order to nurture the area back to how it was before the advent of the European settlers, to how it was when the San people lived with the land. Ecological wounds inflicted in

---

[30] The Garden Route National Park (GRNP) was officially gazetted on 6 March 2009. The motto of the 121 000 hectare National Park is *Conservation Without Boundaries*. No fences encircle the National Park and through corridor initiatives and increased stakeholder involvement, important ecological linkages can be forged in the future.

recent times by weapons, axes, chain saws, poisons and herbicides, can begin to heal. Fynbos will reawaken and emerge in succession in a landscape dominated for decades by pine plantations. With the removal of the farmed exotics and invasive alien tree species, thirsty trees that drank deeply from the water table, long absent springs will flow again and, as I write, have already emerged in some places, clear water seeping, almost with urgency, from the ground. With the removal of the exotics, pioneer tree species such as candlewood, red alder and Cape beech are also emerging, young and vigorous, almost eager, plants. And so are the restios, the favoured fynbos food of the elephants. Once mechanically and manually mowed down because they competed with pine, these plants are growing swiftly upwards, their flower heads swaying in the mountain breeze.

With the rehabilitation of the landscape and natural healing processes, careful planning can then take place for the reintroduction of the wildlife species that up until the past century and a half had historically always belonged here, animals like red hartebeest, mountain zebra, eland, buffalo, and a myriad of other species. It will be like an ecological homecoming.

There will be many challenges ahead, but the path can be seen and walked towards, the long-term conservation of a land that, with its wild denizens, had been dealt devastating blows in the past. And coinciding with these developments, a civil society based environmental project was born, the Eden to Addo Corridor Initiative.

I attended an early meeting about this project and listened with interest to Pam Booth, a dynamic young environmentalist: 'What if we could re-establish ancient elephant migration paths across the southern Cape? What other wildlife will benefit and how would that help to restore the ecological balance?'

Pam's thoughts on the elephants' ancestral pathways potentially being 'living corridors' to link once again the wild lands here reflected my own thoughts and feelings. Today Pam is the project coordinator of the Eden to Addo Corridor Initiative, which strives to create an effective pattern of habitats from the central range of the Knysna elephants to the Addo Elephant National Park, corridors that will ensure ecological connectivity. She works towards these goals with private landowners and stakeholders, as well as provincial and state conservation authorities. The scope of this initiative is limitless.

Conservation scientists today admit that putting a fence around a protected wildlife park or reserve is insufficient to protect the patterns and processes that are naturally required for proper ecological functioning. Like elephants, everything needs space to move. Today more than ever before, this is becoming evident to everyone. In response to climate change particularly, everything, the animals, birds and even plants, must have freedom to move. To be trapped or fragmented by human-defined boundaries such as fences and 'development' spells disaster for the biological diversity that all life, including our own, depends upon. And it is here that a tiny relic elephant population, the free moving Knysna elephants, increasingly symbolises the ecological necessity of corridors, the freedom to move to ensure biological diversity and the survival of species.

Our DNA study was to reveal some exciting surprises. Lori's lab work showed that there are at least five female elephants within the Knysna population. The analysis showed that the females are all related, with the results suggesting two of the females are a first order, or parent-offspring relationship. Therefore a mother and daughter existed, with the other three females being half-siblings. In addition, I knew of the existence of two calves. I was also confident about the existence of the mature (musth) bull, and the Young Bull, though they were not detected in the DNA work. Together, the DNA study and the field evidence suggest that a minimum of nine Knysna elephants roam the forest, fynbos and mountains of the southern Cape. In addition, bolus measurements in the DNA study indicated that all five females are young adults. Indeed, the overall results suggested that we have a small young elephant population. This evidence was contrary to the previously embedded, but unsubstantiated, hypothesis that the Knysna elephants were inevitably a doomed population, made up of old animals that were simply dying out, with few or even no births taking place for several decades. Our study results shocked, even seemingly angered, a few former forestry officials and scientists, presently employed by SANParks, who had long maintained (and had been previously unchallenged) that the Knysna elephants were doomed to extinction. Indeed even as I write, these people are still maintaining negatively that only one Knysna elephant exists, the Matriarch . . .

Just prior to receiving the DNA results Wilfred managed to capture the image of one of the elephants. Late one afternoon Wilfred and Karel came across the elephant in a clearing near the Quar forest. They had been following tracks for most of the day, very distinctive footprints that had come to be familiar to the guards and me for the past four years. Strangefoot.

The elephant was feeding in fynbos on the edge of the forest. As the guards cautiously approached to get a clear view, the warm summer evening breeze drifted and the elephant became aware of their presence. The elephant swung its trunk upwards and probed the air to detect Wilfred and Karel's proximity. This was the first image that Wilfred captured of Strangefoot, her trunk raised and searching.

When I later saw Wilfred's photographs it was evident that Strangefoot was a female, which was what I had suspected for a long time, and that she was about seventeen years old. The images showed a beautiful young adult female elephant in fine condition. And her noticeably rounded hindquarters suggested, to me at least, that Strangefoot might even be in the late stages of pregnancy.

The DNA results also told us that the Knysna elephants and those of Addo are genetically one population. Surprisingly, the genetic diversity of the five Knysna females we had detected was higher than in the Addo elephants. This was intriguing, yet at the same time did not remove reasons to be concerned about the dangers of inbreeding within our little population. The opposite in fact. The size of the Knysna population after all has been small for a long time, and breeding between related individuals reduces the genetic variability of the population and increases the chances that harmful genes will be expressed. Inbreeding reduces the probability that individuals will have the genes needed to adapt to changes in the environment, such as new parasites and diseases, or even changes in climate or available food plants. Clearly, the way ahead to ensure the long-term future of the elephants was to learn about the two bulls (and other possible bulls) that were not detected in the initial DNA work. The fact that we had identified females only did not surprise me too much. In elephant society it is normal for the females to have main range and activity areas, and through the DNA study and the fieldwork, we had identified this range area of the Knysna females.

Bull areas are often in more isolated places, or rather in areas not used extensively by the females and young. Bulls also roam widely, having wider habitat tolerance than the rest of the population. To fully understand the dynamics of the Knysna elephants (and to ensure their long-term survival) work with the males is now imperative. And as I write this, Lori and I have begun DNA research to verify the existence and identification of the Knysna bulls.

Intriguingly, just after Lori's lab work revealed the presence of at least five females within the Knysna population, a totally unexpected source told of several Knysna elephants being seen together one night in farm pastures bordering the southern forest.

I heard of the report, and duly interviewed the man who (with others) claimed to have seen the elephants. Peter, I learnt, had grown up on his parents' farm on the edge of the forest, and clearly knew the area very well. He told me that one evening a few months earlier, he received a radio call from his father that he should come immediately to the farm. Elephants had been seen in the farm pastures close to the Homtini River that snakes southwards from the mountains to the sea.

Peter then saw the elephants for himself. Four, he estimated, were young adults, while one was noticeably larger than the others.

'This is the very first time we have had elephants on the farm. It was an astonishing scene,' Peter said, and remarked that 'the vehicle headlights had not unduly disturbed the elephants'.

Sitting there interviewing Peter, and listening to his story, I felt strongly that this was a very credible account. He had no reason to make up the story. And there were other people there that night who had also seen the elephants.

That evening, news of the elephants circulated on the neighbourhood farm two-way radio network.

'The following morning I received a visit from two (presumably forestry department) officials,' Peter told me at the end of our discussion. 'They asked me not to mention publicly what we had seen the night before in the pastures.'

T W E N T Y - N I N E

My Soul's Land

This is not just sand to cover my bones.
This is my soul's land...

April 2006
South of the Diepwalle forest station, forestry worker Johnny Dlamini stepped off the verge of Petrus Brand Pad to mark a cut line in the dense undergrowth. Selective felling of old forest trees takes place on a rotational basis every ten years in the indigenous forest, and this was what Johnny was marking the cut line for in that portion of the Knysna forest.

As he carefully moved forward Johnny suddenly saw in front of him, partially covered with branches, leaves and creepers, the metal wreckage of an aircraft. For a few seconds he was not sure what he was seeing until he realised that he was staring straight at the skeletal remains of two people strapped into the cockpit of a helicopter.

It was the Bell Jet Ranger that had gone missing in 1999. Just south of Diepwalle, as the pendulum had indicated.

Utterly shocked, Johnny turned to run back to the nearby road and nearly tripped over a third body lying intact and covered in moss just a few feet from the wreckage.

The Macfarlanes' remains were later removed from the crash site and Ian and Frances Macfarlane were buried at the Diepwalle forest station cemetery. Boyd Macfarlane's body was flown to Pretoria to be buried beside his wife. In some ways this was almost a reburial. Robbie Macfarlane, the youngest son of the deceased, commented on what the forest had hidden and then later remarked, 'While it has brought us much pain, it is also a very spiritual place and we are now at peace with what happened here.'[31]

Not long after the burial at Diepwalle, a mere 20 kilometres away to the south-west, the remains of an adult Knysna elephant were discovered. The bones were found just behind a primary dune that overlooks the sand-shifting breakers of the Indian Ocean. How long the bones had lain there, buried in the sand, nobody knows.

The finding – by pure chance – of the helicopter and the elephant, is very symbolic to me. This is a mysterious land with mysterious inhabitants. It is a secret place to respect and to step lightly in. As the first people, the San, once did. It is a humbling place, for what resonates loudly is how little we modern humans know about the ancient interconnected relationships that exist here.

Having damaged this earth, having tainted the water, poisoned the air, and changed the climate, the time has now come to protect at all costs all the last remaining wild places in the world. If we do not do this, those who come after us will be spiritually and environmentally impoverished, with mystery gone and secret places no more than a memory. To me, the remarkable existence today of the Secret Elephants represents hope – even for ourselves.

---

[31] Nicole Schafer, 'Sons at peace after vanished chopper found in forest'. Draft of proposed news article, May 2006.

Acknowledgements

To Knysna forest guards Wilfred Oraai, Karel Maswatie and Paulus Makriga, thank you for sharing with me your knowledge of this spectacular place and your insights about the astonishing elephants. It must be said that the Knysna elephants have a particularly good friend in Wilfred Oraai. His enthusiasm and love for them is boundless, and I think that the elephants themselves know this . . .

Much love to Fransje van Riel. Thank you for your patience and support.

My thanks to Daphne Sheldrick for writing the Foreword to this book. I do not have adequate words to describe what Daphne has contributed to the preservation of the African elephant and our knowledge of these beings.

Many thanks to Professor Keto Mshigeni for the vital work that he is doing. May your ongoing research, and that of your colleagues, in exploring the medicinal wonders of *Ganoderma* bear fruit and provide solutions to the disease that ravages the African continent.

I would like to thank the following who were formerly with the Department of Water Affairs and Forestry, Knysna (and are now with SANParks, Knysna) who assisted me in my endeavours to learn about the Knysna elephants: Len du Plessis, Klaas Havenga, Johan Baardt, Jeffrey Sass, Martin Lucas, Hylton Herd, Cyril Sam, Lietie Sam and Solly Lacminnie. Special thanks, too, to Hylton Herd for letting me use his remarkable photographs of the Knysna elephants.

I much appreciate the cooperation of Connie Jonker and Bradley Jumat, both with MTO, and Jim Parkes of Geo Parkes and Sons, for assistance with the Knysna elephant DNA research project.

During the course of the project I sought the knowledge of many specialists in many fields. I would like to thank the following for sharing their knowledge with me: Margaret Tagwira of The Africa University at Mutare, Zimbabwe; Peter Linder of the Institute for Systematic Botany in Zurich; Margo and George Branch for assistance with mushroom identification; Cindy Engel and her book *Wild Health* for introducing me to the field of *Zoopharmacognosy*; Vivek Menon of the Wildlife Trust of India for information about Asian elephants; Janette Deacon for giving me insights into the last San of these parts; Dr John Santer of the South African Bureau of Standards for undertaking the spring water quality tests; Anna Whitehouse for information on the Knysna elephant's extended family, the elephants of Addo; Ian Redmond for information on elephant habituation and the work of the Mount Elgon Elephant Monitoring Team; Dr Amina for enlightening me on the medicinal use of *G. applanatum* in Uganda; Dr Richard Sullivan of Cancer Research UK; Suzanne Diamond in Canada for the mushroom and tannin work; Andrea Turkalo, who expands our knowledge of the forest elephants in the rainforests of the Central African Republic; Christopher Hobbs from the important field of medicinal mushrooms; Luba in faraway Russia, thanks for the research you did for me there; Debbie Martyr and Jeremy Holden for sharing with me their knowledge of the orang pendek; Addi Longley-Taylor for documenting in detail for me her 'Ele-encounter' of 2001; Antoni Milewski, who undertook important work with the forest guards into the diet of the Kruger orphans; their work began to confirm my early suspicions that the Knysna elephants are not restricted to the forests alone; Chris Roche for allowing me to draw historical insights on people and the elephants from his thesis; Yvette van Wijk of the Southern Cape Herbarium, and IMITHI Medicinal Plant Project; Liezel Mortimer of the Wildlife Action Group (WAG) for sourcing various papers and reports for me.

Margo Mackay, author of the book *The Knysna Elephants and their Forest Home*, sadly passed away before I finished writing this book. Margo, like Wilfred, was another great friend and stalwart supporter of the Knysna elephants. For years Margo, with the Knysna Centre of the Wildlife and Environment Society of South Africa, lobbied to secure the future of the Knysna elephants. She kindly gave me access to her archive material on the Knysna elephants, saying to me, 'I am passing on the baton now, Gareth.'

Thanks also to Don Pinnock, Fiona Macleod, Lydia van der Merwe, Melanie Gosling, Sheree Bega, Jo-Ann Bekker, Liesl Hattingh and many other journalists who wrote about the uplifting story of the 'new' Knysna elephants.

Grateful appreciation to Barnie Barnardo for writing the insightful *Olifant Wêreld* report, and to Julie Carlisle, formerly of the Nature's Valley Trust, for passing on a copy of this from her archives.

Many thanks to Venise Grossman who established my website www.garethpatterson.com back in 2000, and who continues to manage it to this day. The website has been an invaluable tool in creating awareness of my work. In 2007, Venise also kindly produced the splendid web-video on the Knysna elephants that can be viewed on the home page of my site.

My great appreciation to Michael MacIver and all the good people of the Baobab Charity UK. These are young South Africans living in Britain who raise funding for wildlife projects in back home in South Africa. The project vehicle that they obtained for me still serves me well.

Many thanks to Soila Saiyielel and Jed Bird for assisting with the determination of the age of the Knysna calf by comparison with known-aged calves at Amboseli National Park, Kenya, and at Addo Elephant National Park, South Africa.

Thanks also to my friend Nicole Schafer for allowing me to use material from her 'Sons at Peace' story.

Thanks to Gillian Carter. These elephants are like certain memories, never far from one's mind.

In Lyall Watson I discovered a kindred spirit with regard to the Knysna elephants. It is my great regret that he did not read this book. Lyall was a great champion of the Knysna elephants. I and legions of people around the world miss him very much.

Much love and thanks to my special friend Dominique Diane. Dominique also illustrated this book with her beautiful drawings that were partly inspired by our frequent walks together in the forests and the foothills of the mountains during 2007 and 2008.

Thanks to Mark van Wijk, film-maker and good friend, for achieving what he did with the documentary project on the Knysna elephants. Anyone who has seen the documentary, *The Search for the Knysna Elephants*, will attest to how beautifully and sensitively it was filmed.

My thanks to Alison Lowry and everyone at Penguin Books South Africa for embracing the story of the secret elephants. It was great working with Louise Grantham, Claire Heckrath and Reneé Naudé. To Pam Thornley, my editor, it was lovely to be working with you once again.

Great thanks and love to Karin Saks for her comments and advice.

To my friends, Julie Carlisle and Rozanne Savory, heartfelt appreciation and love.

Thanks to Riaan van Niekerk and Stephen van Romburgh of Bytes and Pieces who somehow managed to retrieve a draft version of this book from a computer that had otherwise died . . .

Many thanks to Lori Eggert for collaborating with me so that we could learn more about the elusive Knysna elephants through the important DNA project. Thanks very much, Lori.

Thanks to my brother Stewart Patterson and Petra ten Velde for your invaluable assistance in the field with the second phase of the DNA work, and the ongoing Knysna elephant work.

Many thanks to all the people who hike, cycle, live or work in the forests and mountains, for kindly passing on to me valuable information on the signs of the elephants that they came across over the years.

Last, but certainly not least, I would like to thank Joyce Poole for giving me advice and support and for sharing her knowledge with me right from the very beginning of the Knysna elephant project. I believe that Joyce knows elephants like nobody else. I had been deeply immersed in the lives of lions for a decade and a half before turning to elephants for a while. I therefore left a comfort home of familiarity, switching species after such a long time. Suddenly, I was confronted by large gaps in my knowledge about elephants. And I had thought once that I knew a fair amount about them . . . But Joyce was always at hand to give advice, to fill the many gaps, and this is appreciated very much.

That said, though, any mistakes I may have made in this book concerning elephants and their ways are mine and mine alone!

Gareth Patterson
Knysna 2009

Copyright Acknowledgements

The author would like to thank the following for permission to reproduce copyright material:

Els Dorrat Haaksma and H Peter Linder for permission to quote from their book, *Restios of the Fynbos*, the Botanical Society of South Africa, 2000. Cynthia Moss for permission to quote from her book *Elephant Memories*, Elm Tree Books, 1988. David Jenkins for kind permission to quote from his mother's classic, *The Plains of Camdeboo* by Eve Palmer, London, Collins, 1966. Material from *Jungle Man – the autobiography of Major P J Pretorius* (Resnick's Library of African Adventure, 2001) reproduced by permission of Ralph Roberts of Alexander Books. Appreciation also to Mike Resnick. Material from *Gorillas in the Mist* by Dian Fossey (copyright Dian Fossey 2001), reprinted by permission of A M Heath & Co. Ltd, Authors' Agents. Material from *The Electronic Elephant* by Dan Jacobson (copyright Dan Jacobson 1994), reprinted by permission of A M Heath & Co. Ltd, Authors' Agents. W.W. Norton & Company, Inc for material from *Guns, Germs and Steel* (1997) by Jared Diamond. W.W. Norton & Company, Inc. for material from *Elephantoms* (2003) by Lyall Watson. University of Chicago Press for material from *Year of the Gorilla* (1997) by George Schaller. Little, Brown Book Group for material from *Beauty and the Beast* (Virago 2001) by Carole Jahme. Hodder and Stoughton Ltd for material from *Coming of Age with Elephants* (1996) by Joyce Poole. Keto Mshigeni for material from his paper 'Africa's Mushrooms: a neglected bioresource whose time has come', published in *Discovery and Innovation*, 17 (3/4), 2004. Richard Sullivan, John Smith and Neil Rowan for material from *Medicinal Mushrooms: Their therapeutic properties and current medical usage with special emphasis on cancer treatment* (May 2002) published by

Cancer Research UK. Andre Boshoff for material from 'Elephants in the broader Eastern Cape – An historical overview', in: Kerley, G, Wilson, S & Massey, A (eds), *Elephant Conservation and Management in the Eastern Cape*. Terrestrial Ecology Research Unit (University of Port Elizabeth) Report No 35: 3-15.

Photographic Acknowledgements

The author would like to thank the following for allowing him to use their wonderful photographs in *The Secret Elephants*:

Hylton Herd, Wilfred Oraai and Paulus Makriga of SANParks. Fransje van Riel, my brother Stewart Patterson and Dominique Diane. Sophie Vartan and NHU Africa for the use of the stills from the documentary *The Search for the Knysna Elephants*, and Mark van Wijk who captured these scenes. Hilary Peter for the use of the unique photograph taken by her father Francis William Newdigate in 1940 of a magnificent Knysna bull elephant.

Select Bibliography

Adamson, George (1968). *Bwana Game.* London: Collins Harvill.

Adamson, George (1986). *My Pride and Joy.* London: Collins Harvill.

Babaasa, Dennis (2000). Habitat selection by elephants in Bwindi Impenetrable National Park, south-western Uganda. *African Journal of Ecology,* 38 (2): 116.

Balfour, Daryl & Sharna (1997). *African Elephants: A Celebration of Majesty.* Struik.

Barnardo, Barnie (n d). *Olifant Wêreld* (Elephant World). Nature's Valley Trust Archives.

Barnes, R F W (2001). How reliable are dung counts for estimating elephant numbers? *African Journal of Ecology,* 39 (1): 1-9

Becker, Peter (1985). *The Pathfinders.* London: Viking.

Ben-Shahar, R (1997) Elephants and woodlands in Northern Botswana: How many elephants should be there? *Pachyderm,* 23: 41-43.

Blake, S & Douglas-Hamilton, I (2001). GPS telemetry of forest elephants in Central Africa: results of a preliminary study. *African Journal of Ecology,* 39 (2): 178-186

Blundell, Geoffrey & Lewis-Williams, David (2002). Storm Shelter: An important new rock art find in the southern Drakensberg, *South African Journal of Science* January/February.

Blunt, David E (1963). *Elephant.* London: Neville Spearman. Reprint.

Boonzaier, Emile, Malherbe, Candy, Berens, Penny, & Smith, Andy (1996). *The Cape Herders: a history of the Khoikhoi of Southern Africa* David Phillip/Ohio University Press.

Branch, Margo and George (2001). *Sasol First Field Guide to Mushrooms of Southern Africa,* Struik Publishers.

Bristow, David (text). (1990) *Garden Route.* Struik Publishers.

Bull, Bartle. (1988). *Safari, A Chronicle of Adventure.* London: Viking.

Buss, Irven O (1990). *Elephant Life: Fifteen Years of High Population Density.* Ames: Iowa State University Press.

Cannon, P F, Kirk, P M, Mibey, R K & Siboe, G M. *Microfungus Diversity and Conservation Agenda in Kenya,* Darwin Initiative Project, 1997-2000.

Carter, Nick. *Knysna Elephant Survey. February 1969 – January 1970.* The Wildlife Protection and Conservation Society of South Africa, Eastern Province Branch.

Carter, Nick (1971). *The Elephants of Knysna.* Cape Town: Purnell.

Chang, S T (2004). The Development of the Mushroom Industry in China, with a note on possibilities for Africa. *Discovery and Innovation,* 15 (3/4).

Chang, S T & Mshigeni, K E (2001). *Mushrooms and human health: their growing significance as potent dietary supplements.* Windhoek: University of Namibia.

Cowley, Geoffrey. Now, 'Integrative' Care, *Newsweek,* December 2002.

Cumming, Gordon R (1850). *Five Years of a Hunter's Life in the Far Interior of South Africa,* London.

De Boer, Willem F, Ntumi, Cornelio P, Correia, Augusto U & Mafura, Jorge, M (2000). Diet and distribution of elephant in the Maputo Elephant Reserve, Mozambique. *African Journal of Ecology,* 38 (3): 188-201.

De Watteville, Vivienne (1936). *Speak to the Earth: Wanderings and Reflections among Elephants and Mountains.* London.

Diamond, Suzanne (1996). Hormone Pollution, Synthetic Estrogens and the Cancer Connection. *Alive Magazine.*

Diamond, Suzanne (2000). Beauty in Peril – The Stoltmann Wilderness. *HerbalGram* 48: 50-62.

Dinesen, Isak (1954). *Out of Africa.* London: Penguin Books.

Domisse, E J (1951). The Knysna Elephants. *African Wildlife,* 5 (3). September.

Douglas-Hamilton, Iain and Oria (1975). *Among the Elephants.* London: Collins & Harvill Press.

Douglas-Hamilton, Iain and Oria (1992). *Battle for the Elephants.* London: Doubleday.

Dudley, J P (1996). African Elephants in Coastal Refuges: Postscript. *Pachyderm,* 22 (6).

Eggert, L S, Patterson, G L & Maldonado, J E. The Knysna elephants: a population study conducted using faecal DNA. *African Journal of Ecology,* online version, 2 June 2007.

Eggert, L S, Ramakrishnan, U, Mundy, N I & Woodruff G O S (2000). Polymorphic microsatellite DNA markers in the African elephant (*Loxodonta africana*) and their use in the Asian elephant (*Elephas maximus*). *Molecular Ecology*, 9 (12): 2222-4.

Eltringham, Keith (ed.) (1991). *The Illustrated Encyclopaedia of Elephants*. London: Salamander Books.

Engel, Cindy (2002). *Wild Health*. London: Weidenfeld & Nicolson.

Estes, Richard D (1999). *The Safari Companion: a guide to watching African animals*. Chelsea Green Publishing Company.

Fitzgerald, Beth (1996). *Not Ready for Roundup: Glyphosate Fact Sheet*. Washington: Greenpeace.

Foley, C A H, Papageorge, S & Wasser, S K (2001). Noninvasive Stress and Reproductive Measures of Social and Ecological Pressures in Free-Ranging African Elephants. *Conservation Biology*, 15 (4): 1134-42.

Fossey, Dian (1983). *Gorillas in the Mist*. London: Hodder and Stoughton.

Fourie, Coral (1994). *Living Legends of a Dying Culture*. Cape Town.

Fraser, Michael & McMahon, Liz (1994). *Between Two Shores: Flora and Fauna of the Cape of Good Hope*. Cape Town: David Philip Publishers.

Gary, Romain (1959). *The Roots of Heaven*. Michael Joseph and the Book Society.

Gavron, Jeremy (1993). *The Last Elephant: An African Quest*. HarperCollins

Goodall, Jane (1990). *Through a Window*. London: Weidenfeld & Nicolson.

Gordon, Nicholas (1991). *Ivory Knights: Man, Magic and Elephants*, Hodder and Stoughton.

Groning, Karl & Saller, Martin (1998). *Elephants: A Cultural and Natural History*. Konemann.

Green, Lawrence G (1973). *Great African Mysteries*. Cape Town: Howard Timmins. Reprint.

Green, Lawrence G (1974). *Strange Africa*. Cape Town: Howard Timmins. Reprint.

Green, Lawrence G (1974). *Secret Places*. Cape Town: Howard Timmins. Reprint.

Haaksma, Els Dorrat & H Peter Linder (2000). *Restios of the Fynbos*, Botanical Society of South Africa.

Hanks, John (1979). *A Struggle for Survival*, Struik.

Hoare, Richard E & Du Toit, Johan T (1999). Coexistence between People and Elephants in Africa's Savannas. *Conservation Biology*, 13

(13): 633-9.

Hobbs, Christopher (1996). *Medicinal Mushrooms: An Exploration of Tradition, Healing and Culture,* Santa Cruz: Botanica Press.

Hobbs, Christopher (1999). Calm Your Spirit with the Revered Reishi Mushroom. *Herbs for Health,* Sept-Oct 1999, pp. 40-42.

Houston, D C, Gilardi, J D & Hall, A J (2001). Soil consumption by Elephants might help to minimize the toxic effects of plant secondary compounds in forest browse. *Mammal Review,* 31 (3 & 4): 249-54.

Huffman, M A (2001). Self-Medicative Behavior in the African Great Apes: an Evolutionary Perspective in the Origins of Human Traditional Medicine. *BioScience,* 51 (8): 651-61.

Jacobson, Dan (1994). *The Electronic Elephant.* London: Hamish Hamilton.

Jahme, Carole (2001). *Beauty and the Beasts: Woman, Ape and Evolution.* London: Virago Press.

Jordan, W, Poole J, Sheldrick, D & Gillson, L (1998). *Elephants,* Care for the Wild.

Kangmin, Li (1999). Traditional Use of Mushrooms in China. *ZERI Newsletter,* March.

Kangwana, Kadzo (ed.) (1996). *Studying Elephants.* African Wildlife Foundation.

Kench, John (1987). *The Coast of Southern Africa.* Cape Town: Struik.

Kenine, E, Comstock, Samuel, Wasser, K & Ostrander, Elaine A (2000). Polymorphic microsatellite DNA loci identified in the African Elephant (*Loxodonta africana*). *Molecular Ecology,* 9 (7): 1004-6.

Kenyon, Georgina, *Mushrooms: the new medicine,* BBC News, Health. December 2001.

Kerley, Graham, Wilson, Sharon & Mossey, Ashley (eds) (2002). *Elephant Conservation and Management in the Eastern Cape,* Terrestrial Ecology Research Unit Report No 35, University of Port Elizabeth.

Kinloch, Bruce (1968). The Mysterious Giants of the Knysna Forest, *Animal.*

Koen, J H (1983). Seed Dispersal by the Knysna Elephants. *South African Forestry Journal,* No 124: 56-8.

Koen, J H (1988). Trace Elements and some other nutrients in the diet of the Knysna elephants. *South African Journal of Wildlife Research,* 18

(3): 109-10.

Koen, J H, Hall-Martin, A J & Erasmus, T (1988). Macronutrients in plants available to the Knysna, Addo and Kruger National Park Elephants. *South African Journal of Wildlife Research*, 18 (2): 69-71.

Lawley, Lisa (1991). *Elephants: A Battle for Survival*. London: Headline.

Leakey, Richard, E (2001). *Wildlife Wars: My battle to save Kenya's elephants*. New York: St Martins Press.

Livingstone, David (1857). *Missionary Travels*, London: Ward, Lock and Company Limited.

Luhke, Roy & de Moor, Irene (eds) (1998). *The Field Guide to the Eastern and Southern Cape Coasts*. University of Cape Town Press.

Mackay, Margo (1991). *The Knysna Elephants and Their Forest Home*. Wildlife and Environment Society of South Africa, Knysna Centre.

Marais, J S (1957). *The Cape Coloured People: 1652-1937*. Johannesburg: Witwatersrand University Press.

Martin, N T (1995). The Problem Elephants of Kaele: A Challenge for Elephant Conservation in Northern Cameroon. *Pachyderm*, No 19: 26-32.

Masson, Jeffrey & McCarthy, Susan (1994). *When Elephants Weep: The Emotional Lives of Animals*. Jonathan Cape.

Matthee, Dalene (1984). *Circles in a Forest*. Cape Town: Tafelberg Publishers.

Matthee, Dalene (1985). *Fiela's Child*. Cape Town: Tafelberg Publishers.

Matthee, Dalene (1987). *The Mulberry Forest*. Cape Town: Tafelberg Publishers.

Maybury-Lewis, David (1992). *Millennium: Tribal Wisdom and the Modern World*. London: Viking.

Mayell, Hillary. Satellites Reveal How Rare Elephants Survive Desert. *National Geographic* News, 26/9/2003.

Mbiti, John S (1969). *African Religions and Philosophy*. Heinemann Educational Books.

Meschino, James (2002). *Reishi Mushroom Extract and Immune Support*, ChiroWeb.com.

Metelerkamp, Sanni (1963). *George Rex of Knysna*. Cape Town: Howard Timmins.

Milewski, A V (2002). Elephants and Fynbos, *Veld and Flora*, March.

Milewski, A V (2002). Diet of the African Elephant at the Edge of the Fynbos Biome, *Pachyderm*, July.

Mindell, Earl (1991). *Vitamin Bible*. New York: Warner Books, Inc.

Mizuno, Takashi (1996). *Studies on Bioactive Substances and Medicinal Effects of Reishi (Ganoderma lucidum)*. Shizuoka University.

Moore, Randall J & Munnion, Christopher (1989). *Back to Africa*. Johannesburg: Southern Books.

Moss, Cynthia (2000). *Elephant Memories*. University of Chicago Press.

Mostert, N (1992). *Frontiers*. Pimlico, 1992.

Mowszowski, Ruben (2001). Last of the Rainmakers. Geographical magazine (UK), August.

Mshigeni, K E (2004). Africa's Mushrooms: a neglected bioresource whose time has come. *Discovery and Innovation*, 17 (3/4).

Mshigeni, K E, Chang S T & Gwanama C (2003). Surprises, scientific charm, socio-economic potential, and possibilities in the mushroom world. *Discovery and Innovation*, 15: 1-7.

Mutwa, Credo (1966). *Indaba, My Children*. London: Kahn and Averill.

Mutwa, Credo (1996). *Song of the Stars: The Lore of a Zulu Shaman*. New York: Station Hill Openings, Barrytown Ltd.

Mutwa, Credo (1996). *Isilwane*. Johannesburg: Struik.

Nchanji, Anthony Chifu & Plumptre, Andrew J (2001). Seasonality in elephant dung decay and implications for censusing and population monitoring in south-western Cameroon. *African Journal of Ecology*, 39 (1): 24-32.

Newton, Michael (2002). *Savage Girls and Wild Boys: a history of feral children*. London: Faber and Faber.

Nicholson-Lord, David (2003). *Elephantine Miracle*. BBC Wildlife. July.

Nimmo, Arthur (1976). *The Knysna Story*. Cape Town: Juta and Company Ltd.

Omer-Cooper, J D (1994). *History of Southern Africa*. UK: James Currey Publishers.

Palmer, Eve (1966). *The Plains of Camdeboo*. London: Collins.

Paterson-Jones, Colin (1992). *Garden Route Walks*. Johannesburg: Struik.

Patterson, Gareth (1989). *Cry for the Lions*. Aftex.

Patterson, Gareth (1994). *Last of the Free*. London: Hodder and Stoughton.

Patterson, Gareth (1995). *With my Soul Amongst Lions*. London: Hodder and Stoughton.

Patterson, Gareth (1998). *Dying to be Free: The canned lion scandal*.

Johannesburg: Viking Penguin.

Patterson, Gareth (2001). *To Walk with Lions*. Rider Books.

Patterson, Gareth (2004). Knysna Elephants and Medicinal Mushrooms: A Case of Self-Medication that has Contributed to the Survival of a Relic Population? *Discovery and Innovation*, 16 (1/2): 1-4.

Payne, Katy (1998). *Silent Thunder: The Hidden Voice of Elephants*. London: Weidenfeld & Nicolson.

Phillips, J F V (1925). The Knysna Elephants – a brief note on their history and habits. *South African Journal of Science*, 22: 287-93.

Pinnock, Don (2004). Mythical Monsters of the Ancient Forest, *Getaway*, 15 (3) March.

Poole, Joyce (1996). *Coming of Age with Elephants*, London: Hodder and Stoughton.

Pretorius, P J (1947). *Jungle Man*. London: George G. Harrap and Company Ltd.

Pringle, J A (1982). *The Conservationists and the Killers*. Cape Town: TV Bulpin & Books of Africa.

Reader, John (1997). *Africa, a biography of the continent*. London: Hamish Hamilton.

Riley, H (1963). *Families of Flowering Plants of Southern Africa*. University of Kentucky Press.

Roche, Chris (1997). *The Elephants at Knysna* and *The Knysna Elephants, from exploitation to conservation: man and elephants at Knysna, 1856-1920*, University of Cape Town.

Schaller, George (1964). *The Year of the Gorilla*. University of Chicago Press.

Selous, F C. *Travel and Adventure in South East Africa*. Books of Rhodesia, 1971. Reprint of 1883 edition.

Seydack, A H W, Vermeulen, C & Huisamen, J (2000). Habitat quality and the decline of an African elephant population: Implications for conservation. *South African Journal of Wildlife Research*, 30 (1): 34-42.

Skead, C J (1980). *Historical mammal incidence in the Cape Province, Volume 1: The western and northern Cape*. Department of Nature & Environmental Conservation. Cape Provincial Administration.

Skead, C J (1980). *Historical mammal incidence in the Cape Province, Volume 2: The eastern half of the Cape Province, including the Ciskei, Transkei, and East Griqualand*, Department of Nature & Environmental

Conservation, Cape Provincial Administration.

Skinner, J D & Smithers, R H N (1990). *The Mammals of the Southern African sub region*. University of Pretoria.

Smit, Adriann W (2003). Medicinal Mushrooms: major medicinal mushrooms and their use as nutriceuticals and dietary supplements. *The South African Journal of Natural Medicine*, 10: 13-15.

Smith, John, Rowan, Neil J & Sullivan, Richard (2002). *Medicinal Mushrooms: Their Therapeutic Properties and Current Medical Usage with Special Emphasis on Cancer Treatments*. Cancer Research UK, University of Strathclyde. May.

Somerville, Keith. *West African elephants 'separate' species*. BBC News Online. 26/9/2002.

Stone, Richard (2002). *Mammoth: the Resurrection of an Ice Age Giant*. London: Fourth Estate.

Sullivan, Brenda (2001). *Africa Through the Mists of Time*. South Africa: Covos Day Books.

Tapson, Winifrid (1961). *Timber and Tides*, General Litho.

Teow, S S (1997). *Cultivation, Utilization and Medicinal Effects of* Ganoderma lucidum *in Malaysia*. MARA Institute of Technology.

Theal, G McCall (ed.) (1919). *History and Ethnography of Africa, South of the Zambesi, before 1795,* 3 vols.

Thesen, H P. Encounters with Knysna Elephants. *African Wildlife*.

Thornton, Allan & Curry, Dave (1991). *To Save an Elephant: The Undercover Investigation into the Illegal Ivory Trade*. Doubleday.

Turkalo, Andrea & Fay, J Michael (1995). Studying Forest Elephants by Direct Observation. *Pachyderm*, 20: 45-54.

Uhland, Vicky (2003). Medicinal Mushrooms Come Out of the Dark. *Natural Foods Merchandiser*, XXIV (7): 28-30.

Underwood, Anne & Liu, Melinda (2000). Learning from China. *Newsweek*. December.

Van der Merwe, Isak (1997). *The Knysna and Tsitsikamma forest*. Department of Water Affairs and Forestry.

Van der Post, Laurens (1958). *The Lost World of the Kalahari*. London: Hogarth Press.

Van der Westhuizen, G C A & Eicker, Albert (1994). *Mushrooms of Southern Africa*, Johannesburg: Struik.

Von Breitenbach, F (1984). *Southern Cape Forests and Trees*, Government Printer.

Von Breitenbach, F (1985). *Southern Cape Tree Guide.* Department of Environment, Forestry Branch.

Walsh, Peter D & White, Lee J T (1999). What It Will Take To Monitor Forest Elephant Populations, *Conservation Biology,* 13 (5): 1194, October.

Wasser, S P & Weis A L (1999). Medicinal properties of substances occurring in higher Basidiomycetes mushrooms, *International Journal of Medicinal Mushrooms,* 1: 31-62.

Watson, Lyall (2000). *Jacobson's* Organ. New York: W W Norton & Company.

Watson, Lyall (2003). *Elephantoms,* Johannesburg: Viking Penguin.

Watt, J M & Breyer-Brandwijk, M G (1962). *The Medicinal and Poisonous Plants of Southern and Eastern Africa.* E & S Livingstone Ltd.

Western, David (1997). *In the Dust of Kilimanjaro.* Washington DC: Island Press.

Whitehouse, Anna M & Hall-Martin, Anthony J (2000). Elephants in Addo Elephant National Park, South Africa: reconstruction of the population's history. *Oryx,* 34: 46-55.

Whitehouse, Anna M & Irwin, Pat (2000). *A Guide to the Addo Elephants.* Rhodes University, IFAW.

Williams, Heathcote (1989). *Sacred Elephant.* London: Jonathan Cape.